DISNEYLAND PARIS FIRST - TIME VISIT GUIDE 2025

ANGELA G. BRIEN

COPYRIGHT

Copyright © 2025 Angela G. Brien
All rights reserved.

Disclaimer: This guide is an independent publication and is not affiliated with, authorized, or endorsed by Euro Disney Associés S.A.S., Disneyland Paris, The Walt Disney Company, or any of their affiliates.

While every effort has been made to ensure the accuracy and completeness of the information contained in this guide, the author and publisher accept no responsibility for any errors, omissions, or inaccuracies.

Table of Contents

Introduction
What is Disneyland Paris?
History and Significance
Location and Overview
Why Visit Disneyland Paris?

CHAPTER 1
Planning Your Visit
Best Time to Visit
How Many Days to Spend
Disneyland Paris Annual Events and Festivals
Weather and Seasonal Tips

CHAPTER 2
Getting There
By Air (Charles de Gaulle, Orly, Beauvais Airports)
By Train (Eurostar, RER, and TGV)
By Car (Driving Directions and Parking Options)
Shuttle Services and Private Transfers

CHAPTER 3
Accommodation Options
Official Disneyland Paris Hotels
Partner Hotels Near Disneyland Paris
Staying in Central Paris vs. Near the Park
Tips for Choosing the Right Accommodation

CHAPTER 4
Tickets and Packages
Types of Tickets (1-Day, Multi-Day, Annual Pass)
Park Hopper vs. Single Park Tickets
Booking Packages: Hotel + Tickets
Discounts and Promotions

CHAPTER 5
Disneyland Paris Parks Overview
Disneyland Park
Main Attractions and Themed Lands
Rides for Kids, Families, and Thrill Seekers
Walt Disney Studios Park
Top Attractions and Zones
Latest Additions (e.g., Avengers Campus, Frozen Land)

CHAPTER 6
Top Attractions and Experiences
Must-Ride Attractions
Parades and Shows
Meet-and-Greets with Disney Characters
Nighttime Spectaculars: Disney Dreams! and Illuminations

CHAPTER 7
Dining at Disneyland Paris
Table-Service Restaurants
Quick-Service and Snacks
Character Dining Experiences
Food Allergies and Special Diets
Insider Tips for Dining Reservations

CHAPTER 8
Shopping and Souvenirs
Top Shops in the Parks
Unique Souvenirs and Merchandise
Tips for Budget-Friendly Shopping

CHAPTER 9
Disneyland Paris for Kids
Rides and Attractions for Little Ones
Baby Care Centers and Child-Friendly Services
Stroller Rentals and Accessibility

Accessibility and Services
Accessibility for Guests with Disabilities
Language Considerations (English vs. French)
Mobile App and Park Navigation
Wi-Fi, Charging Stations, and Lockers

CHAPTER 10
Tips for Beating the Crowds
Using Genie+ or FastPass Alternatives
Early Entry and Extra Magic Hours
Quiet Times and Less Busy Seasons

CHAPTER 11
Budgeting for Disneyland Paris
Cost Breakdown: Tickets, Accommodation, Food, and Extras
Money-Saving Tips and Hacks
Budget-Friendly Dining and Shopping

CHAPTER 12
Exploring Beyond Disneyland Paris
Val d'Europe and La Vallée Village Shopping
Day Trips to Paris and Versailles
Other Attractions Near Disneyland Paris

CHAPTER 13
FAQs and Insider Tips
Commonly Asked Questions
Cultural Differences to Be Aware Of
Tips from Disneyland Paris Veterans

CHAPTER 14
Emergency Information
First Aid and Medical Assistance
Lost and Found Services
Contact Numbers and Useful Apps

CHAPTER 15
Printable Resources
Park Maps and Layout
Daily Planner Template
Packing Checklist
Most Visited Places in Paris
1 Week Detailed Itinerary

Introduction

What is Disneyland Paris?

Disneyland Paris is Europe's most popular theme park resort, combining world-class entertainment, immersive storytelling, and the enchanting magic of Disney. Opened on April 12, 1992, it was the first Disney park in Europe and remains one of the top tourist destinations on the continent. The resort is made up of two theme parks: **Disneyland Park**, which features iconic lands like Fantasyland and Adventureland, and **Walt Disney Studios Park**, dedicated to the art of filmmaking and Disney franchises. In addition, Disneyland Paris offers a vibrant shopping and entertainment district called **Disney Village** and numerous themed hotels.

History and Significance

The idea of a European Disney resort was conceived in the 1980s, as Disney sought to expand its magical experiences beyond North America and Asia. France was chosen over other European countries due to its central location, accessibility, and strong tourism industry.

The park faced challenges during its early years, with initial resistance from the French public and financial difficulties. However, strategic changes in marketing, attractions, and overall guest experience helped turn it into a resounding success. Today, Disneyland Paris celebrates its role as a cultural bridge, blending Disney's iconic Americana with European charm.

Significant milestones include:
- **1992**: Grand opening as Euro Disney Resort.
- **2002**: Opening of Walt Disney Studios Park.
- **2022**: Celebrations of the 30th anniversary, with new shows and expansions.
- **Ongoing**: Major investments in expansions like the Avengers Campus and Frozen-themed land.

Location and Overview

Disneyland Paris is located in **Marne-la-Vallée**, a suburban area approximately **32 kilometers (20 miles)** east of central Paris. This strategic location allows for easy access via public transport, car, and international travel hubs like Charles de Gaulle Airport.

The resort covers **4,800 acres**, including:
- **Disneyland Park**: The main theme park with a fairy-tale castle, classic Disney attractions, and themed lands like Main Street, U.S.A., Frontierland, Adventureland, Fantasyland, and Discoveryland.
- **Walt Disney Studios Park**: A film-themed park with zones dedicated to Marvel superheroes, Pixar animations, and the magic of cinema.
- **Disney Village**: A bustling area with shops, restaurants, and entertainment options.
- **Seven Themed Hotels**: Each offering a unique ambiance, from the luxurious Disneyland Hotel to the wild-west-themed Hotel Cheyenne.

Why Visit Disneyland Paris?

Disneyland Paris is a must-visit destination for countless reasons:

- ❖ **Immersive Disney Magic**: It's the only Disney resort in Europe, offering a magical experience with iconic attractions, beloved characters, and stunning shows.
- ❖ **Unique European Touch**: Disneyland Paris blends Disney's American charm with European cultural influences, such as its intricately designed Sleeping Beauty Castle (Le Château de la Belle au Bois Dormant) and gourmet dining options.
- ❖ **World-Class Entertainment**: Visitors can enjoy jaw-dropping parades, nighttime spectaculars, and seasonal events that make every visit unique.
- ❖ **Expanding Attractions**: Recent additions, like the **Avengers Campus**, and upcoming expansions ensure that Disneyland Paris remains a cutting-edge destination.
- ❖ **Family-Friendly Atmosphere**: Perfect for visitors of all ages, from thrilling roller coasters for adventure seekers to gentle rides and character encounters for kids.
- ❖ **Proximity to Paris**: It's an excellent add-on to a Parisian vacation, offering a magical escape just a short train ride from the French capital.
- ❖ **Seasonal Celebrations**: From Halloween to Christmas, Disneyland Paris transforms into a seasonal wonderland with themed decorations, shows, and experiences.

Disney fan, a thrill-seeker, or someone looking for a family-friendly getaway, Disneyland Paris offers a magical experience you'll never forget.

Disneyland Paris

At the heart of the magic lies the breathtaking Sleeping Beauty Castle, making Disneyland® Park the ultimate dream destination with five captivating lands. It's where the tales of princesses, pirates, adventurers, and space voyagers spring to life. Embark on an exciting journey through **Discoveryland**, **Fantasyland**, **Frontierland**, **Adventureland**, and **Main Street, U.S.A.**, all sprinkled with a touch of Disney enchantment!

Did you know? Sleeping Beauty Castle has fascinating French inspirations! Its design draws influence from Mont-Saint-Michel and the intricate castles featured in *Les Très Riches Heures du Duc de Berry*. And those golden snails escaping from the kitchens? Who doesn't love a bit of quirky charm?

What Awaits You Inside Disneyland:
- **41 Attractions**
- **33 Restaurants**
- **17 Shows & Entertainments**
- **36 Shops**

Walt Disney Studios Park

Dive into an adventure-filled world at Walt Disney Studios® Park, where the magic of cinema comes alive!

Here, you can immerse yourself in the exhilarating stories of Disney, Pixar, and Marvel. It's also the home of the **Marvel Avengers Campus**, a fully immersive zone packed with exciting experiences for aspiring heroes of all ages.

For adrenaline seekers and dreamers alike, **The Hollywood Tower Hotel** is a must-visit. Dare to take on the haunted elevator ride of **The Twilight Zone Tower of Terror™**? With three spine-tingling experiences to conquer, it's a thrilling adventure you'll want to repeat!

What Awaits You Inside Walt Studio:
- 12 Attractions
- 10 Restaurants
- 14 Shows & Entertainment
- 10 Shops

Disney Village

Discover a lively hub for shopping, dining, and entertainment! Just a short stroll from the Disney Parks, Disney Village offers an energetic atmosphere brimming with themed restaurants, bars, unique shops, a cinema, and even one of the world's largest tethered balloons. It's the perfect spot for families to grab a meal, unwind with a drink, and find the perfect Disney keepsake.

Plus, the best part? **Entry to Disney Village is absolutely free!**

You'll find a variety of dining options, including popular favorites like **Rainforest Café**, **Starbucks Coffee**, **Vapiano**, **Five Guys**, **The Royal Pub**, and even **McDonald's**.

What Awaits You Inside Disney Village:
- 17 Shops
- 15 Restaurants
- 1 Disney Village Web Radio

Disney Premier Access Ultimate

Take your Disneyland Paris experience to the next level with **Disney Premier Access Ultimate**! This feature lets you skip the regular line once for all eligible Disney Premier Access attractions (excluding Orbitron), so you can enjoy the day at your own pace without worrying about time slots.

How It Works
1. **Access with Ease**:
    - Purchase Disney Premier Access Ultimate and get quicker access to all eligible attractions.
    - While it doesn't guarantee immediate boarding, it minimizes your wait time significantly.
2. **Mobile Convenience**:
    - Log into the **Disneyland® Paris Mobile App** with your Disney Account.
    - Obtain a QR code and scan it at the dedicated entrance for each attraction to enter the fast lane.
3. **For Kids Under 3**:
    - Children under 3 don't need Disney Premier Access Ultimate but must be accompanied by an adult with the pass.

Important Notes
- Availability is subject to the open attractions at the time of booking.
- A valid Disney® Park ticket is required to use Disney Premier Access Ultimate.

Preferred Access to Shows & Parades
- **Exclusive Seating**: Secure your spot at popular indoor stage performances, which are open to all but can fill up quickly.
- **Viewing Areas**: Reserve a special spot for the renowned Disneyland® Park parade or nighttime spectacular for an unforgettable view.

How to Book:
These options are only available via the **Disneyland Paris Mobile App**. Guests must log in or create a Disney Account to purchase tickets for the shows or parades.

Disney PhotoPass™+

Capture every magical moment with **Disney PhotoPass™+**. Professional Disney photographers are stationed at select Disney Character Encounters, Magic Shot spots, and rides with photo capture systems.

Benefits:
- **Unlimited Photos**: Gather unlimited photos on a single PhotoPass card.
- **10-Day Activation**: Once activated, the card remains valid for 10 days.
- **One-Year Online Access**: Download your photos anytime from DisneyPhotoPass.eu for up to one year.

Cost: £76.23

Disney VIP Tours

For the ultimate Disney experience, opt for a **VIP Tour**, featuring a personal guide and unparalleled access to the magic of the parks.

Tour Details:
- Available for groups of up to **10 Guests**.

- Enjoy a **6-hour guided visit** packed with incredible perks.

VIP Perks:
- **Quick Access to Attractions**: Skip the lines and enjoy multiple visits to your favorite rides.
- **Exclusive Viewing Spots**: Prime locations for shows and parades.
- **Character Meet-and-Greets**: Shorter wait times to meet Mickey Mouse, Disney Princesses, and more.

Leave the planning to your VIP guide for a stress-free, magical adventure!

Dog-Friendly Stays at Disney Davy Crockett Ranch

If you're planning a magical getaway with your furry friend, **Disney Davy Crockett Ranch** offers select **dog-friendly cabins** with everything you need for a comfortable stay.

Key Details
- **Limit Per Cabin**: One dog per cabin.
- **Welcome Pack**: Includes a dog collar, a disposable mat, five poop bags, and two Disney-branded bowls (1).
- **Crates Available**: Guests can borrow a crate from reception to leave their dog alone in the cabin (deposit required).
- **Fee**: £26.90 per dog, per night.

Important Notes
- **What's Not Included**: Dog food and access to the kennels at Disney® Parks. (Kennels have limited

spots, no advance booking, and additional charges apply.) Dog essentials like food, toys, and accessories are available at the shop in Disney Davy Crockett Ranch.

Terms & Conditions for Dogs

1. **Breed Restrictions**: Dogs classified as dangerous under French law (Category 1 or 2) are not allowed.
2. **Vaccination Requirements**:
    - An up-to-date vaccination card must be presented at check-in.
    - Dogs must have received a rabies vaccination at least **21 days before arrival**.
    - Dogs must be identifiable via microchip or tattoo.
3. **Supervision & Leashes**: Dogs must be on a leash and supervised by an adult when outside the cabin.
4. **Restricted Areas**: Dogs are not allowed in public buildings, including the Reception and dining areas.
5. **Cabin Types**: Dog-friendly accommodations are available in select **Trapper** and **Premium Cabins** only.

How to Book

To reserve a dog-friendly cabin, call Disney Experts at **03448 008 898** (standard call rates apply, and costs may vary by network). The Disney team will check availability, provide additional information, and add the booking to your record.

10 Simple Steps to Plan Your Disneyland Paris Adventure for First-Timers

Planning your first visit to **Disneyland Paris** can feel overwhelming, but with these **10 easy steps**, you'll be ready to experience the magic and see the stunning Sleeping Beauty Castle under blue skies with perfect clouds floating by.

Step 1: Familiarize Yourself with the Disneyland Paris App

The Disneyland Paris app is your ultimate planning companion! Start by downloading it from your app store and signing in (or creating) a Disney account. Here's what to do next:

- Link your tickets and reservations to the app for easy access.
- Explore the park map and attractions to build excitement.
- Create a wishlist of rides, shows, and characters you don't want to miss.

💡 **Pro Tip**: If you're a Disney+ subscriber, you can use the same login for the app!

Step 2: Set Your Budget

Before booking anything, take time to plan your budget. List the key expenses like:

- Hotel and park tickets
- Travel costs (flights, train, or driving)
- Food, drinks, and souvenirs

Keep your budget flexible by adding placeholders for unexpected expenses.

🪙 **Pro Tip**: Check out discounts and money-saving tips to keep costs down without sacrificing the magic.

Step 3: Choose the Right Hotel
From luxurious Disney hotels to nearby off-site options or cozy Airbnbs, there's a range of accommodations to suit every budget. Consider:
- Staying on-site for perks like early park access.
- Off-site hotels with free shuttles for affordability.
- Booking through a trusted platform for the best deals.

Step 4: Plan Your Travel to Disneyland Paris
Decide how you'll get there:
1. **Eurostar Train**: Fast, convenient, and direct to Marne-la-Vallée station.
2. **Flights**: Land at Charles de Gaulle Airport and take a shuttle to the parks.
3. **Driving**: Ideal for families and those wanting to bring more luggage.

Each option has its pros and cons, so choose what works best for your location and budget.

Step 5: Pick Your Park Tickets
Decide how many days you want to spend at the parks and whether you'll need a Park Hopper ticket. These tickets allow you to visit both Disneyland Park and Walt Disney Studios on the same day.

✏ **Pro Tip**: Packages that bundle hotels and tickets can often save money, so compare options carefully.

Step 6: Book Your Trip
Now that you've chosen your travel, hotel, and tickets, it's time to book! Use your budget as a guide and book everything online or through a Disney travel expert.

Step 7: Plan Your Meals
Disneyland Paris offers a variety of dining experiences, from quick-service meals to themed dining with characters.
- Use the Disneyland Paris app to view restaurant menus and make reservations.
- Consider whether the Disneyland Paris Meal Plan fits your needs—it's available for on-site guests.

🍽 **Pro Tip**: Popular restaurants like Auberge de Cendrillon (with Disney princesses) require advance reservations.

Step 8: Create a Park Day Plan
With so much to see and do, it helps to have a loose itinerary:
- Prioritize must-do rides, shows, and character meet-and-greets.
- Plan breaks for meals, snacks, and rest time to avoid burnout.

Step 9: Pack Wisely
Make a detailed packing list, including:
- Weather-appropriate clothing and comfortable shoes.
- Essentials like sunscreen, rain gear, and portable chargers.
- A park bag with snacks, water, and first-aid basics.

🎒 **Pro Tip**: Tailor your packing to the season you're visiting. Winter trips may need warm layers, while summer requires light clothing and sun protection.

Step 10: Countdown to Magic!
As your trip approaches, embrace the excitement!
- Watch Disney movies to get in the spirit.
- Create a fun countdown calendar.
- Plan thoughtful souvenirs or gifts to bring home.

CHAPTER 1

Planning Your Visit

Best Time to Visit

Choosing the best time to visit Disneyland Paris depends on your preferences for crowd levels, weather, and seasonal events. Here's a breakdown of what to expect:

1. **Low Seasons (Mid-January to Mid-March, Mid-September to Mid-November):**
    - **Pros:** Fewer crowds, shorter wait times for rides, and lower accommodation costs.
    - **Cons:** Some rides and attractions may be closed for maintenance.
    - Best for those looking for a quieter, budget-friendly experience.
2. **Peak Seasons (Mid-July to August, Christmas, and Easter Holidays):**
    - **Pros:** Longer park hours, full entertainment schedules, and all attractions open.
    - **Cons:** High crowds, longer wait times, and higher ticket/accommodation prices.
    - Ideal for families and those who want the full Disneyland Paris experience.
3. **Seasonal Events (Halloween and Christmas):**
    - Halloween (October): Features spooky decorations, themed shows, and character costumes.
    - Christmas (Mid-November to Early January): A magical experience with festive decorations, holiday parades, and winter-themed attractions.

- Best for those looking to enjoy unique holiday-themed celebrations.

How Many Days to Spend

The ideal duration for your visit depends on how much you want to explore:

1. **One Day**
   - Suitable if you're short on time and only plan to visit one park.
   - Focus on key attractions and shows in either **Disneyland Park** or **Walt Disney Studios Park**.
   - Recommended for those on a tight schedule or making a day trip from Paris.
2. **Two Days**
   - Ideal for visiting both parks: one day for Disneyland Park and another for Walt Disney Studios Park.
   - Allows time for major attractions, shows, and dining without feeling rushed.
3. **Three or More Days**
   - Perfect for a relaxed experience, revisiting favorite attractions, and exploring Disney Village.
   - Allows flexibility to enjoy parades, nighttime shows, and seasonal events without rushing.

Disneyland Paris Annual Events and Festivals

Disneyland Paris hosts several annual events that make each season special. Here are the highlights:

1. **Disneyland Paris Pride (June):**
   - A colorful celebration of inclusivity with a special parade, live music, and themed attractions.
2. **Disneyland Paris Run Weekend (September):**

- A family-friendly marathon event with races for all ages and Disney-themed medals.
3. **Halloween Festival (October):**
    - Spooky decorations, villain meet-and-greets, and Halloween-themed shows.
    - Special events like the Disney Halloween Party with exclusive attractions and entertainment.
4. **Disney Enchanted Christmas (Mid-November to Early January):**
    - Holiday-themed parades, tree-lighting ceremonies, and festive decor throughout the parks.
5. **New Year's Eve Party (December 31):**
    - An exclusive celebration with extended park hours, live music, and a spectacular fireworks display.
6. **Seasonal Mini-Festivals:**
    - Spring: Character meet-and-greets and flower-themed shows.
    - Summer: Extended hours and additional performances.

Weather and Seasonal Tips

Disneyland Paris experiences varied weather throughout the year, so it's important to plan accordingly:

1. **Spring (March to May):**
    - **Weather:** Mild with occasional rain (10–18°C/50–64°F).
    - **Tips:** Pack a light jacket, umbrella, and comfortable walking shoes.
2. **Summer (June to August):**
    - **Weather:** Warm and sunny (18–26°C/64–79°F).

- **Tips:** Use sunscreen, stay hydrated, and take advantage of shaded rest areas. Early park entry is recommended to beat the heat and crowds.
3. **Autumn (September to November):**
    - **Weather:** Cooler with occasional showers (10–20°C/50–68°F).
    - **Tips:** Bring layers and be prepared for changing weather. Enjoy seasonal decorations and events like Halloween.
4. **Winter (December to February):**
    - **Weather:** Cold, sometimes snowy (2–7°C/36–45°F).
    - **Tips:** Wear warm layers, gloves, and waterproof shoes. Christmas decorations add a magical touch to the parks.

No matter when you visit, planning ahead for weather, events, and crowd levels ensures a magical and stress-free experience at Disneyland Paris!

CHAPTER 2

Getting There

Disneyland Paris is located in **Marne-la-Vallée**, approximately 32 kilometers (20 miles) east of Paris. It is easily accessible by various modes of transportation, whether you're arriving from another country, elsewhere in France, or Paris itself. Below are detailed options to help you plan your journey:

By Air
If you're flying into France, Disneyland Paris is well-connected to three major airports:
1. **Charles de Gaulle Airport (CDG):**
    - **Distance to Disneyland Paris:** Approximately 40 kilometers (25 miles).
    - **Travel Time:** 35–45 minutes by car or direct train.
    - **Transportation Options:**
        - **TGV Train:** A high-speed train connects CDG to Marne-la-Vallée/Chessy station (next to Disneyland Paris) in just 10 minutes.
        - **Shuttle Services:** Disneyland Paris offers a Magical Shuttle bus from CDG to the resort. The journey takes about 60 minutes.
        - **Taxis or Private Transfers:** A convenient but more expensive option, taking approximately 35–45 minutes.

17

2. **Orly Airport (ORY):**
    - **Distance to Disneyland Paris:** Approximately 47 kilometers (29 miles).
    - **Travel Time:** 45–60 minutes by car or bus.
    - **Transportation Options:**
        - **Magical Shuttle Bus:** Direct service from Orly to Disneyland Paris. Travel time is about 60 minutes.
        - **RER Train:** Take the Orlyval shuttle to Antony station, transfer to RER B to Châtelet-Les Halles, and then connect to RER A to Marne-la-Vallée/Chessy. Total travel time: ~90 minutes.
        - **Private Transfers or Taxis:** Faster but more costly, taking around 45 minutes.
3. **Beauvais-Tillé Airport (BVA):**
    - **Distance to Disneyland Paris:** Approximately 120 kilometers (75 miles).
    - **Travel Time:** 90–120 minutes by car.
    - **Transportation Options:**
        - **Shuttle Bus + Train:** Take the Beauvais Airport Shuttle to Paris (Porte Maillot), then connect via metro or RER A to Marne-la-Vallée/Chessy.
        - **Private Transfers:** The most convenient but expensive option, taking about 90 minutes.

By Train

Disneyland Paris is well-served by an excellent rail network, with direct connections to its **Marne-la-Vallée/Chessy** train station, located just a short walk from the parks.

1. **Eurostar (from the UK):**

- Direct trains operate from **London St Pancras International** to Marne-la-Vallée/Chessy in about **2 hours and 45 minutes**.
- Seasonal and weekend services are available, particularly during school holidays.
- Luggage services are streamlined for families and large groups.

2. **TGV (from France and Europe):**
   - High-speed trains connect major French cities (e.g., Lyon, Marseille, Bordeaux) and European destinations (e.g., Brussels, Amsterdam) directly to Marne-la-Vallée/Chessy.
   - Travel times vary but are typically between 1–4 hours depending on the departure location.

3. **RER (from Paris):**
   - **RER Line A** connects central Paris to Disneyland Paris in about 35–45 minutes.
   - Major departure stations include **Châtelet-Les Halles**, **Gare de Lyon**, and **Nation**.
   - Trains run every 10–20 minutes, making it the most frequent and cost-effective option for those staying in Paris.

By Car

Driving to Disneyland Paris is straightforward, with ample parking and clear signage along the way.

1. **Driving Directions:**
   - From Paris: Take the **A4 (Autoroute de l'Est)** eastbound and follow signs for Disneyland Paris (exit 14).
   - From Other Regions: Use a GPS or follow motorway signs for Marne-la-Vallée.

- Approximate drive times:
    - Paris to Disneyland Paris: 45 minutes
    - Lyon: 4 hours
    - Brussels: 3 hours
2. **Parking Options:**
    - **Standard Parking:** Located near the parks; costs approximately €30 per day.
    - **Preferred Parking:** Closer to the park entrances; costs around €45 per day.
    - **Hotel Guests:** Free parking at official Disneyland Paris hotels.
    - **Electric Vehicles:** Charging stations are available in the main parking area.
    - **Disabled Parking:** Dedicated spaces are available near the entrances with proper identification.

Shuttle Services and Private Transfers

For a hassle-free experience, consider shuttle services or private transfers, which offer door-to-door convenience.

1. **Magical Shuttle (Official Disney Service):**
    - Operates between CDG/Orly Airports and Disneyland Paris hotels.
    - Comfortable buses with luggage space and child-friendly seating.
    - Booking in advance is recommended.
2. **Private Transfers:**
    - Private cars or minivans can be pre-booked to take you directly from airports or train stations to your hotel or the parks.
    - Ideal for families, groups, or those with a lot of luggage.

- Costs vary but typically range from €70–€150 one-way, depending on the vehicle size and pick-up location.
3. **Rideshare Apps and Taxis:**
    - Apps like **Uber** and traditional taxis are available but can be more expensive during peak times.
    - Expect to pay around €50–€100 from central Paris or CDG Airport.
4. **Hotel Shuttles (for Partner Hotels):**
    - Many partner hotels near Disneyland Paris offer free or low-cost shuttle services to the parks.
    - Check with your hotel for schedules and availability.

Whichever mode of transport you choose, Disneyland Paris is designed to be easily accessible, ensuring that your magical adventure starts as soon as your journey begins!

Magical Shuttle Transfer

Transfers & Connections

The **Magical Shuttle** offers convenient daily transfers between **Paris-Orly** and **Paris-Charles-de-Gaulle** airports to Disney Hotels (excluding **Disney Davy Crockett Ranch**) and the Disney Parks on arrival and departure days.

Key highlights:
- Direct transfers between **Paris airports**, Disney Parks, and Disney Hotels (except Disney Davy Crockett Ranch).

- Connections via the **Marne-la-Vallée/Chessy bus station** for Partner Hotels and Les Villages Nature Paris.

Transfer Details
1. **Partner Hotels**
   - Customers need to switch buses at **Marne-la-Vallée/Chessy bus station** (Disney Parks).
   - A **free shuttle** connects the station and Partner Hotels.
2. **Les Villages Nature Paris**
   - Transfers also require a switch at **Marne-la-Vallée/Chessy station**.
   - A **fare-paying public bus** is available for the final leg.

Additional Information
- **E-Ticket System**
  - One e-ticket per journey is issued for all passengers in the booking (including children under 3 years old).
- **Disney Express Service**
  - The Magical Shuttle stops at the **Marne-la-Vallée/Chessy bus station**, a short walk from the Disney Parks.
  - If customers book the **Disney Express Luggage Service**, they should disembark at this stop, just 2 minutes from the Disney Express desk.
- **Departure Day Advice**
  - Customers are advised to catch their shuttle at least **3 hours before their latest airport check-in time**.

- **Timetables**
  - Visit www.MagicalShuttle.co.uk for the latest schedules.

Pricing (Per Journey)
- **From/To Paris-Charles-de-Gaulle and Orly Airports**
  - **Adult:** £21.52
  - **Child (3-11 years):** £9.86
  - **Free for children under 3**, as long as they are accompanied by a paying adult.
- Approximate journey time: **1 hour** (varies based on traffic and drop-off location).
- **Free Wi-Fi** on board.

Booking Options
- The **Magical Shuttle** service can be added during the booking process.
- Guests with reduced mobility can reserve a specially adapted transfer vehicle up to **2 working days** before departure.
  - For details, email **contact@magicalshuttle.fr**.

Important Notes
1. Children under 3 travel free but must be accompanied by an adult who has booked the service.
2. Prices are subject to exchange rates at the time of booking. For the latest pricing, check when making the reservation.

This service ensures a seamless start and end to your Disneyland Paris adventure!

Disney Express Luggage Service

Save time and jump straight into the magic of Disneyland Paris! The **Disney Express Luggage Service** allows you to drop off your bags at **Marne-la-Vallée/Chessy train station** and head directly to the parks, while your luggage is delivered to your Disney® Hotel.

How It Works
When You Arrive
1. **Drop Off Your Bags**
    - Visit the **Disney Express counter** located on the first floor of Marne-la-Vallée/Chessy train station.
    - Service hours: **7:45 AM to 9:00 PM**.
    - Bags will be transferred directly to your Disney® Hotel (except **Disney Davy Crockett Ranch**).
2. **Pre-Check-In and Tickets**
    - Complete your **hotel pre-check-in** at the counter.
    - Collect your **Disney Park tickets** and head straight into the fun!

When You Are Leaving

1. **Hotel Luggage Drop-Off**
    - On departure day, drop off your luggage at your hotel's luggage room before **11:00 AM**.
    - Your bags will be sent to the **Disney Express counter** at Marne-la-Vallée/Chessy station.
2. **Pick Up Your Bags**
    - Collect your luggage from the **Disney Express counter** between **1:00 PM and 9:00 PM**.

- Enjoy the parks worry-free until it's time to leave!

Important Details
- **Eligibility**
  - Available exclusively for guests staying at a Disney Hotel or select Partner Hotels (excluding **Disney Davy Crockett Ranch** and **Les Villages Nature Paris**).
- **Safety Restrictions**
  - Some items, like jewelry, laptops, cameras, strollers, and scooters, cannot be transferred.
- **Availability**
  - Limited availability. Make sure to book in advance.

Pricing
- **Price Per Person (Return Trip): £16.14**
  - **Free for children under 3** when accompanied by a paying adult.
  - Prices may vary based on exchange rates; confirm pricing when booking.

Transfer Tips
- This service is available for all hotel guests arriving at **Marne-la-Vallée/Chessy station**, regardless of your travel method (train, **Magical Shuttle**, or other transportation).
- Make sure your travel times align with the **Disney Express counter hours** for a smooth experience.

The **Disney Express Luggage Service** ensures a hassle-free start and end to your magical adventure at Disneyland Paris!

CHAPTER 3

Accommodation Options

Experience the Magic Day and Night

Explore the enchanting world of Disney Hotels.

Many of these accommodations boast swimming pools, fitness facilities, children's play zones, complimentary parking, and even a Disney souvenir delivery service—making relaxation a breeze even when you're not exploring the Disney Parks. Plus, they all provide free parking at the Disney Parks' Guest Parking.

For a truly immersive Disney experience, staying at a Disney Hotel is a must. Whether you're dreaming big or sticking to a budget, there's a magical option to suit everyone, each telling its own distinct Disney story. Some hotels even offer exclusive suites and club rooms with premium perks like private check-in and access to a lounge serving breakfast and afternoon tea.

Official Disneyland Paris Hotels
Staying at an official Disneyland Paris hotel comes with exclusive benefits, such as Extra Magic Time (early park entry), complimentary shuttle services, and Disney-themed ambiance.

Overview of Each Hotel:

Disneyland Hotel (5-star):

- Theme: Victorian elegance and luxury.
- Location: Directly at the entrance to Disneyland Park, offering unparalleled convenience.
- Key Features: Spacious rooms, fine dining, a luxurious spa, and VIP park views. Ideal for those seeking a premium experience.

The reimagined five-star Disneyland® Hotel is now open, standing as the crown jewel of Disneyland® Paris.

Ever fantasized about living like royalty in a magical land? Now's your chance! With its own dedicated entrance to Disneyland® Park and stunning views, this hotel delivers an unparalleled royal experience in the perfect location. The hotel celebrates Disney's royal stories, blending classics like *Beauty and the Beast*, *Cinderella*, and *Sleeping Beauty* with modern favorites such as *Frozen* and *Moana*. Step into a world where you can relive these tales and create your own magical memories.

And it's all paired with playful, five-star luxury that only Disney can provide.

Rooms and Suites

Enjoy elegantly designed rooms inspired by Disney's timeless stories, all while ensuring ultimate comfort. For an elevated stay, opt for a Deluxe Room, Castle Club Room, or Signature Suite, offering exclusive benefits like personalized check-in and private lounge access for gourmet breakfasts and afternoon tea.

Dining

Delight in exceptional dining experiences. Dine with Disney Princesses and princes at **La Table de Lumière**, or feast on a lavish buffet with Mickey, Minnie, and friends at the **Royal Banquet**. End your day with a floral-inspired cocktail at the **Fleur de Lys Bar**.

Activities

Pamper yourself with a day of relaxation at the **Crystal Pool & Health Club** or indulge in luxurious treatments at the **Disneyland® Hotel Spa by Clarins***. Young guests can enjoy enchanting activities at the **Royal Kids Club**, while treasure hunters can shop for exclusive keepsakes at the **Royal Collection Boutique**.

Disney's Hotel New York – The Art of Marvel (4-star):

- Theme: Modern, Marvel superhero-inspired decor with New York City aesthetics.
- Location: ~10-minute walk or a short shuttle ride to the parks.
- Key Features: Marvel artwork, themed suites, indoor/outdoor pools, and character meet-and-greets.

Immerse yourself in the world's first Marvel art-themed hotel, a modern masterpiece infused with New York City charm.

This hotel bridges the dynamic connection between NYC and Marvel, blending Manhattan sophistication with superhero excitement. With over 350 original Marvel artworks by more than 110 artists adorning its walls, the hotel feels like a sleek Upper East Side gallery—with an epic Marvel twist.

Rooms and Suites

Stay in contemporary, Marvel-inspired rooms featuring bold superhero art. For a luxurious touch, upgrade to an **Empire State Club room or suite**, which includes perks like private check-in and access to a lounge offering gourmet breakfast and afternoon tea.

Dining

Indulge in the flavors of the Big Apple. Savor fine Italian cuisine at the **Manhattan Restaurant**, or soak in the bustling New York vibe at the **Downtown Restaurant**. For drinks with a view of superheroes in action, visit the **Skyline Bar**, and for craft beer, organic wine, or artisanal coffee, head to the **Bleecker Street Lounge**.

Activities

Marvel fans of all ages can enjoy thrilling activities. Capture memorable moments at the **Super Hero Station**, where you can pose with your favorite hero in a Marvel-themed setting. Unleash your creativity at the **Marvel Design Studio**, learning how to craft your own Marvel artwork. Get active at the **Hero Training Zone**, an outdoor fitness area. For relaxation, the **Metro Pool & Health Club** offers heated indoor and outdoor pools, a sauna, steam room, whirlpool, and state-of-the-art fitness facilities.

Step into a world of wonder, luxury, and unforgettable Disney magic!

Disney's Newport Bay Club (4-star):

- Theme: Nautical charm inspired by 1920s seaside mansions.
- Location: ~15-minute walk or a short shuttle ride to the parks.
- Key Features: Indoor/outdoor pools, elegant dining, and lakefront views.

Wake up in a charming seaside retreat filled with Disney magic!

Set along the picturesque shores of Lake Disney, this elegant 1920s-inspired mansion showcases classic New England style with a sprinkle of Mickey's playful charm. This four-star resort offers delectable dining options, a cozy bar, refreshing swimming pools, a sauna, a steam room, and impeccable service.

After an exciting day at the Disney Parks, unwind in this tranquil haven. With visits from Mickey, Minnie, and friends, the **Little Sailors' Club** for kids, and the parks just a short walk away, Disney's Newport Bay Club offers everything you need for a memorable vacation.

Rooms and Suites

Relax in light-filled, nautical-themed rooms that capture the essence of Mickey's maritime adventures. For an enhanced experience, upgrade to a **Compass Club room or suite**, where you'll enjoy premium perks like exclusive check-in and access to a private lounge serving gourmet breakfast and afternoon tea.

Dining

Savor New England cuisine with a Mediterranean flair at the **Yacht Club**. For a variety of delicious flavors, explore the nautical-inspired menu at **Cape Cod**. End your day with a refreshing drink at **Captain's Quarters**, the perfect place to unwind after a magical adventure.

Activities

There's fun for every member of the family!
- **For Adults:** Relax at the **Nantucket Pool and Health Club**, which features heated indoor and outdoor pools, a sauna, a steam room, a whirlpool, and a fitness center.
- **For Kids:** Young guests can meet sailor Mickey, Minnie, and their friends for unforgettable photo opportunities.
- **Shopping:** Visit the **Bay Boutique** for vacation essentials and exclusive Disney souvenirs.

With its enchanting seaside ambiance, top-tier amenities, and signature Disney touches, Disney's Newport Bay Club is the perfect setting for a magical getaway!

Disney's Sequoia Lodge (3-star):

- Theme: Rustic forest retreat with cozy, lodge-style decor.
- Location: ~15-minute walk or a short shuttle ride to the parks.
- Key Features: Indoor pool with a slide, woodland-themed rooms, and warm fireplaces in the common areas.

Nestled among towering sequoia trees, this lodge offers a warm and cozy escape for families and adventurers alike.

Rooms and Suites

Experience rustic charm with beautifully themed rooms inspired by national parks and Disney's *Bambi*. The friendly staff ensures a welcoming and memorable stay.

Dining

Treat yourself to a hearty meal at **Hunter's Grill**, featuring an all-you-can-eat menu perfect for explorers. Afterward, unwind by the impressive stone fireplace at the **Redwood Bar and Lounge**, where you can sip on your favorite drinks and plan the next day's adventures.

Activities

- **Quarry Pool and Health Club**: Enjoy heated indoor and outdoor pools, water games, slides, and a fitness center.
- **Kids' Corner**: Let the little ones have fun in a dedicated play area.
- **Character Meet-and-Greets**: Spot Goofy, Max, or their pals during your stay.
- **Shopping**: Visit the **Northwest Passage boutique** for magical keepsakes and essentials.

Disney's Hotel Cheyenne (2-star):

- Theme: Wild West cowboy town.
- Location: ~20-minute walk or a short shuttle ride to the parks.
- Key Features: Western-themed rooms, bunk beds for kids, and immersive decor.

Step into a lively Wild West town for a budget-friendly and exciting stay!

Rooms

Stay in cowboy-themed accommodations inspired by Woody and Jessie from Disney and Pixar's *Toy Story*. The playful decor makes it a hit for kids and adults alike.

Dining

- **Chuck Wagon Cafe**: Relish smoky ribs and chicken straight from the grill in a Western-inspired setting.
- **Red Garter Saloon**: Enjoy live country music and toast to your adventures with your favorite beverage.
- **Starbucks®**: Take a break with a refreshing coffee or snack.

Activities

- **Kids' Corner**: A space for young ones to play and enjoy.
- **Pixar Character Encounters**: Meet Woody, Jessie, and their friends for unforgettable moments.
- **General Store**: Stock up on daily essentials and magical souvenirs.

Disney's Hotel Santa Fe (2-star):

- Theme: Southwest USA with **Cars** movie decor.
- Location: ~20-minute walk or a short shuttle ride to the parks.
- Key Features: Budget-friendly rooms with Pixar's Cars-themed details and relaxed dining options.

Embrace the road trip vibe with a stay at this fun-filled retreat inspired by Route 66 and Disney and Pixar's *Cars*. Perfect for travelers on a budget!

Rooms

Stay in *Cars*-themed rooms that immerse you in the world of Lightning McQueen and Mater. A great choice for families and fans of the movies.

Dining

- **La Cantina**: Indulge in a Mexican-style all-you-can-eat buffet that's perfect for a family feast.
- **Rio Grande Bar**: Relax with a drink in a New Mexico-themed setting after a long day.
- **Starbucks**: Recharge with coffee or a quick snack.

Activities

- **Kids' Corner**: A fun spot for children to play and enjoy.
- **Disney Character Encounters**: Meet iconic characters for magical photo opportunities.
- **Trading Post Boutique**: Shop for road trip essentials and unique Disney souvenirs to take home.

Disney's Davy Crockett Ranch

Escape to the great outdoors in this charming American frontier-themed village, perfect for guests of all ages seeking adventure and relaxation.

Cabins

Stay in self-catering cabins adorned with delightful touches of Ranger Mickey magic. Each cabin comes with:

- A private deck featuring a picnic table and BBQ area.
- Convenient private parking right outside your cabin.

Dining

- **Crockett's Tavern**: Savor a hearty all-you-can-eat buffet with your fellow adventurers.
- **Crockett's Saloon**: Unwind with a drink and enjoy a game of pool in a rustic and cozy setting.
- **Alamo Trading Post**: Stock up on fresh ingredients for your BBQ or grab some souvenirs and essentials.

Activities

- **Blue Springs Pool**: Make a splash in this heated indoor pool, complete with a waterfall, river, and whirlpool.
- **Sports and Recreation**: Enjoy an indoor tennis court, a mini-golf course, and outdoor play areas scattered around the ranch.
- **Family Fun**: The ranch offers plenty of space for outdoor activities and exploring, perfect for nature lovers.

Important Note

Disney's Davy Crockett Ranch is only accessible by car. There is no shuttle service to the Disney Parks or the Marne-la-Vallée/Chessy train station, so make sure to plan your transportation accordingly.

This rustic retreat offers the perfect blend of wilderness charm and Disney magic, making it an ideal getaway for families and groups seeking a unique and relaxing experience!

Les Villages Nature Paris (Eco-Resort):

- Theme: Nature and sustainability with a focus on relaxation.
- Location: ~15-minute drive from the parks (shuttle available).
- Key Features: Spacious cottages/apartments, an indoor water park, and outdoor activities.

2. **Key Amenities and Themes:**
   - **Themed Rooms:** All Disney hotels feature immersive decor that matches their themes, from superhero suites to cowboy bunk beds.
   - **Dining Options:** Onsite restaurants range from casual buffets to fine dining, often with Disney character appearances.
   - **Pools and Recreation:** Many hotels offer pools, spas, and play areas for kids.
   - **Exclusive Benefits:** Extra Magic Time, free shuttle services, and priority reservations for dining and experiences.

Partner Hotels Near Disneyland Paris

Partner hotels are non-Disney properties that are approved by Disneyland Paris. They offer more affordable options while maintaining high standards and proximity to the resort.

1. **Top Partner Hotels:**

- **Vienna House Dream Castle Hotel:** Castle-themed hotel with family-friendly amenities, including spacious rooms, a pool, and shuttle services to the parks.
- **Vienna House Magic Circus Hotel:** Circus-themed decor with colorful interiors, a pool, and entertainment for kids.
- **B&B Hotel at Disneyland Paris:** Budget-friendly with modern, minimalist rooms and free breakfast.
- **Radisson Blu Hotel:** Upscale option with a golf course and modern amenities, ideal for adults or business travelers.

2. **Key Features:**
   - Complimentary shuttle buses to Disneyland Paris.
   - Family-friendly amenities like pools, play areas, and larger rooms.
   - Competitive pricing compared to Disney hotels.

Staying in Central Paris vs. Near the Park

Both options have unique advantages and cater to different types of travelers:

1. **Staying Near the Park:**
   - **Pros:**
     - Short travel time to the parks, allowing more time for attractions and less stress.
     - Access to exclusive Disney benefits (for official hotels).
     - Perfect for families with young children or those focusing solely on Disneyland Paris.

- **Cons:**
  - Less access to Parisian attractions and dining.
  - Limited nightlife and cultural activities compared to the city center.

2. **Staying in Central Paris:**
   - **Pros:**
     - Access to iconic landmarks, world-class dining, and rich culture.
     - Ideal for combining a Disney trip with a broader Parisian vacation.
   - **Cons:**
     - Longer travel time (30–45 minutes by RER A).
     - May require an early start to fully enjoy the parks.

Tips for Choosing the Right Accommodation
1. **Budget:**
   - Choose a Disney Value Hotel (Santa Fe or Cheyenne) or a Partner Hotel for cost savings.
   - If budget allows, splurge on the Disneyland Hotel or Marvel Hotel for convenience and luxury.
2. **Travel Party:**
   - Families with young children may prefer official Disney hotels for Extra Magic Time and themed rooms.
   - Groups of friends or adults may find partner hotels or Paris accommodations more suitable.
3. **Purpose of Visit:**

- If Disneyland Paris is your primary focus, stay as close to the park as possible.
- If you want to explore both Disneyland Paris and Paris itself, consider splitting your stay.

4. **Special Needs:**
   - Look for hotels with accessibility options, such as elevators, wheelchair-friendly rooms, and proximity to shuttle services.
5. **Book Early:**
   - Official hotels and partner properties fill up quickly, especially during peak seasons and special events.

With a wide range of accommodations available, you can tailor your Disneyland Paris trip to fit your budget, preferences, and travel plans while ensuring a magical and memorable stay.

CHAPTER 4

Tickets and Packages Guide for Disneyland Paris

Disneyland Paris offers a variety of ticketing options and packages to suit the needs of every visitor. Whether you're planning a single day visit or a multi-day vacation, this detailed guide to help you choose the right options and make the most of your experience.

1. Types of Tickets
a. 1-Day Tickets
- **Description**: Perfect for visitors with limited time who want to explore Disneyland Paris in a single day.
- **Options**:
    - **Dated Tickets**: Available for specific dates and usually cheaper.
    - **Flexible Tickets**: Can be used on any date but cost slightly more.
- **Includes Access to**: Disneyland Park or Walt Disney Studios Park (or both, if Park Hopper is selected).
- **Best For**: Day-trippers or those passing through Paris with limited time.

b. Multi-Day Tickets
- **Description**: Ideal for visitors who wish to explore the parks over several days.
- **Options**:
    - Available for 2, 3, or 4 days.

- o Can be used on consecutive days or, in some cases, non-consecutive days.
- **Includes Access to**: Both Disneyland Park and Walt Disney Studios Park (Park Hopper included).
- **Best For**: Families and travelers who want to fully experience all the attractions, shows, and parades.

c. Annual Passes
- **Description**: Best for frequent visitors, offering unlimited access and exclusive benefits throughout the year.
- **Types of Annual Passes**:
    1. **Discovery Pass**: Budget-friendly, ideal for occasional visitors with some blackout dates.
    2. **Magic Flex Pass**: Offers more flexibility with fewer blackout dates.
    3. **Magic Plus Pass**: Includes almost no blackout dates and additional perks like free parking.
    4. **Infinity Pass**: Top-tier pass with unlimited access, exclusive discounts, VIP privileges, and premier parking.
- **Best For**: Frequent visitors or locals who want to enjoy the parks year-round.

2. Park Hopper vs. Single Park Tickets
a. Single Park Tickets
- **Description**: Grants access to either Disneyland Park or Walt Disney Studios Park for the day.
- **Pros**:
    - o More affordable than Park Hopper tickets.
    - o Allows you to focus on one park's attractions and entertainment.
- **Best For**: Visitors with limited time or a specific park in mind.

b. Park Hopper Tickets
- **Description**: Allows unlimited access to both Disneyland Park and Walt Disney Studios Park on the same day.
- **Pros**:
  - Flexibility to switch between parks throughout the day.
  - Ideal for those wanting to experience the highlights of both parks.
- **Cons**:
  - More expensive than Single Park Tickets.
- **Best For**: Visitors with multi-day tickets or those wanting a comprehensive experience in one day.

3. Booking Packages: Hotel + Tickets
a. What's Included in a Package
- Accommodation at a Disneyland Paris hotel or partner hotel.
- Multi-day park tickets (Park Hopper included).
- Optional add-ons like dining plans, airport transfers, or VIP tours.

b. Benefits of Booking a Package
- **Convenience**: Everything is arranged in one booking.
- **Savings**: Bundling hotel and tickets often results in discounts compared to booking separately.
- **Exclusive Perks**:
  - Early Park Access (Extra Magic Time) for Disneyland hotel guests.
  - Themed rooms and immersive experiences.
  - Proximity to the parks, reducing travel time.

c. How to Book
- Directly through the **Disneyland Paris website** or app.
- Via travel agencies specializing in Disney vacations.

- Use official promotions and deals for the best prices.

4. Discounts and Promotions
a. Seasonal Offers
- Disneyland Paris frequently offers seasonal deals, especially during off-peak times.
- Examples:
    - Discounts on multi-day tickets.
    - Free dining plans with select packages.
    - Reduced prices on hotel + ticket bundles.

b. Group Discounts
- Special rates for groups of 12 or more.
- Ideal for school trips, corporate outings, or large family gatherings.

c. Special Rates for Certain Guests
- **Children**: Reduced rates or free tickets for children under a certain age (varies by promotion).
- **Residents**: Discounts for French or European residents.
- **Annual Passholders**: Discounts on additional tickets, dining, and merchandise.

d. Early Booking Discounts
- Book tickets or packages in advance to secure lower prices and availability.

e. Partner Deals
- Look for collaborations with airlines, rail services (like Eurostar), or credit card companies offering exclusive discounts.

f. Last-Minute Deals
- Occasionally available for hotel stays and tickets, particularly during off-peak periods.

Tips for Maximizing Your Disneyland Paris Experience
1. **Plan Ahead**: Book tickets and packages in advance to lock in the best deals.
2. **Choose the Right Ticket**: Consider how many days you need and whether Park Hopper is worth it for your itinerary.
3. **Take Advantage of Perks**: Stay at a Disney hotel for Extra Magic Time and easy access to the parks.
4. **Monitor Promotions**: Keep an eye on the official Disneyland Paris website for discounts and seasonal offers.
5. **Be Flexible**: If possible, visit during off-peak times to save money and avoid crowds.

With these options and tips, you can tailor your Disneyland Paris experience to suit your preferences, budget, and schedule.

CHAPTER 5

Disneyland Paris Parks Overview

Disneyland Paris is home to two distinct parks, **Disneyland Park** and **Walt Disney Studios Park**, each offering a unique experience. Below is a detailed overview of **Disneyland Park**, its attractions, themed lands, and ride recommendations for all types of visitors.

Disneyland Park
Disneyland Park is the heart of Disneyland Paris, a magical wonderland where iconic Disney stories come to life. Opened in 1992, it features the enchanting **Sleeping Beauty Castle (Le Château de la Belle au Bois Dormant)** as its centerpiece. The park is divided into five immersive themed lands, each with its own unique atmosphere, attractions, and entertainment.

Main Attractions and Themed Lands
1. **Main Street, U.S.A.**
    - **Theme:** Nostalgic turn-of-the-20th-century American town.
    - **Highlights:**
        - Horse-drawn streetcars, vintage vehicles, and charming shops.
        - **Disney Stars on Parade** and seasonal events often begin here.
        - **Dining:** Enjoy classic American treats at **Casey's Corner** or tea at **Victoria's Home-Style Restaurant**.

- **Don't Miss:** End the day with the **Disney Dreams! Nighttime Spectacular**, a stunning fireworks and projection show viewed from Main Street.

2. **Adventureland**
   - **Theme:** Exotic locales filled with exploration and adventure.
   - **Highlights:**
     - **Pirates of the Caribbean:** A swashbuckling boat ride through pirate-infested waters.
     - **Indiana Jones™ and the Temple of Peril:** A thrilling roller coaster for adrenaline junkies.
     - **Adventure Isle:** Perfect for families, with caves, bridges, and a pirate ship to explore.
   - **Dining:** Try Moroccan-inspired cuisine at **Restaurant Agrabah Café**.

3. **Frontierland**
   - **Theme:** The Wild West, with rugged landscapes and gold-rush adventures.
   - **Highlights:**
     - **Big Thunder Mountain:** A high-speed mine train roller coaster through a desert canyon.
     - **Phantom Manor:** A spooky, immersive haunted house with a Western twist.
     - **Thunder Mesa Riverboat Landing:** A relaxing paddleboat cruise with scenic views.

- Dining: Savor BBQ and Tex-Mex dishes at **The Lucky Nugget Saloon**.

4. **Fantasyland**
   - **Theme:** A fairy-tale kingdom inspired by classic Disney stories.
   - **Highlights:**
     - **It's a Small World:** A gentle boat ride celebrating cultures worldwide.
     - **Peter Pan's Flight:** Fly over London in a magical pirate ship.
     - **Alice's Curious Labyrinth:** Explore a whimsical maze based on *Alice in Wonderland*.
     - **Sleeping Beauty Castle:** Explore the castle's interior galleries and the dragon's lair below.
   - **Dining:** Treat yourself to French pastries at **Au Chalet de la Marionnette**.

5. **Discoveryland**
   - **Theme:** A futuristic world inspired by science fiction and exploration.
   - **Highlights:**
     - **Star Wars Hyperspace Mountain:** A high-speed, space-themed roller coaster.
     - **Buzz Lightyear Laser Blast:** A family-friendly interactive shooting game.
     - **Orbitron:** A spinning ride offering panoramic views of the park.
   - **Dining:** Enjoy futuristic vibes and burgers at **Café Hyperion**.

Rides for Kids, Families, and Thrill Seekers

Disneyland Park offers a variety of attractions suited to different age groups and preferences:

1. **Rides for Kids:**
    - **It's a Small World:** Whimsical and colorful, perfect for young children.
    - **Dumbo the Flying Elephant:** A gentle ride offering magical views from above.
    - **Le Carrousel de Lancelot:** A classic merry-go-round in Fantasyland.
2. **Rides for Families:**
    - **Pirates of the Caribbean:** Suitable for all ages, with mild thrills and incredible visuals.
    - **Buzz Lightyear Laser Blast:** A fun interactive experience for kids and adults.
    - **Peter Pan's Flight:** A magical journey that delights both children and grown-ups.
3. **Rides for Thrill Seekers:**
    - **Big Thunder Mountain:** A high-speed roller coaster through a Wild West mine.
    - **Indiana Jones™ and the Temple of Peril:** Features sharp turns, steep drops, and inversions.
    - **Star Wars Hyperspace Mountain:** A roller coaster with an exciting galactic twist, complete with stunning effects.

Disneyland Park combines nostalgia, wonder, and thrills, ensuring that visitors of all ages can create magical memories. Whether you're exploring pirate coves, venturing into space, or soaking in the fairy-tale charm of Fantasyland, this park has something special for everyone!

Walt Disney Studios Park

Walt Disney Studios Park, the second theme park in Disneyland Paris, opened in 2002 and offers a behind-the-scenes glimpse into the world of movies, television, and animation. With a mix of thrilling rides, immersive zones, and live entertainment, it's a haven for film enthusiasts and Disney fans alike. The park is divided into themed zones, each offering unique attractions, shows, and dining options.

Top Attractions and Zones
1. **Front Lot**
   - **Theme:** The golden age of Hollywood, complete with art deco architecture and movie magic nostalgia.
   - **Highlights:**
     - **Studio 1:** A Hollywood-themed indoor street with restaurants, shops, and a glamorous ambiance.
     - Great photo opportunities with vintage props and the iconic Walt Disney Studios globe at the entrance.
2. **Production Courtyard**
   - **Theme:** Behind-the-scenes exploration of TV and cinema production.
   - **Highlights:**
     - **The Twilight Zone Tower of Terror™:** A thrilling free-fall ride with a chilling storyline and stunning visuals.
     - **Stitch Live!:** An interactive comedy show featuring Stitch, great for kids and families.

- **CinéMagique:** A nostalgic show celebrating the history of cinema (check if available during your visit, as it often rotates).

3. **Toon Studio**
   - **Theme:** The magic of Disney animation, featuring beloved characters and stories.
   - **Highlights:**
     - **Crush's Coaster™:** A spinning roller coaster inspired by *Finding Nemo* that combines underwater visuals with exciting twists and turns.
     - **Ratatouille: The Adventure:** A 4D trackless ride that shrinks you to the size of a rat and takes you on a culinary adventure through Gusteau's restaurant.
     - **Cars ROAD TRIP:** A relaxing and fun journey into the world of *Cars*, featuring memorable scenes and characters.

4. **Worlds of Pixar**
   - **Theme:** Pixar's iconic films brought to life with vibrant, family-friendly attractions.
   - **Highlights:**
     - **Slinky Dog Zigzag Spin:** A gentle spinning ride perfect for younger guests.
     - **RC Racer:** A thrilling half-pipe roller coaster featuring the lovable RC from *Toy Story*.

- **Toy Soldiers Parachute Drop:** A drop tower ride with a military theme, offering fun views of the park.

5. **Avengers Campus** (Latest Addition, Opened in 2022)
   - **Theme:** A high-tech, superhero training facility where you can interact with Marvel heroes.
   - **Highlights:**
     - **Spider-Man W.E.B. Adventure:** An interactive ride where you help Spider-Man capture rogue Spider-Bots using gesture-based technology.
     - **Avengers Assemble: Flight Force:** A thrilling roller coaster featuring Iron Man and Captain Marvel, complete with high-speed action and stunning visuals.
     - **Character Encounters:** Meet heroes like Iron Man, Black Panther, Captain Marvel, and more during impromptu or scheduled appearances.
   - **Dining Options:**
     - **Pym Kitchen:** A unique dining experience with oversized and miniature dishes inspired by Ant-Man and the Wasp.
     - **Stark Factory:** A casual eatery with a superhero-industrial theme.

6. **Frozen Land** (Opening Soon, Scheduled for 2024-2025)
   - **Theme:** Immerse yourself in the world of *Frozen*, featuring a re-creation of Arendelle.
   - **Highlights (Planned):**

- **Frozen Ever After Ride:** A magical boat ride through iconic scenes from the movies, with state-of-the-art animatronics and music.
- **Character Meet-and-Greets:** Meet Anna, Elsa, Olaf, and other beloved characters in an enchanting setting.
- **Arendelle Village:** Shops, dining, and interactive experiences that immerse guests in *Frozen*'s Nordic-inspired world.

7. **Backlot (Transitioning to Avengers Campus)**
   - Previously home to stunt shows and the Rock 'n' Roller Coaster, this area has been transformed into part of the **Avengers Campus**.

Latest Additions: Focus on Avengers Campus and Frozen Land

1. **Avengers Campus (Opened 2022):**
   - The most significant addition to Walt Disney Studios Park in recent years, Avengers Campus offers thrilling rides, live-action hero encounters, and immersive Marvel-themed dining. It's a must-visit for superhero fans.
   - Cutting-edge technology in rides like **Spider-Man W.E.B. Adventure** sets a new standard for interactive attractions.
   - Themed merchandise is available at shops like the **Mission Equipment Store**, perfect for Marvel collectors.
2. **Frozen Land (Coming Soon):**

- Frozen Land promises to be a highlight of Walt Disney Studios Park, providing guests with an all-new immersive experience.
- The expansion will feature breathtaking architecture and landscaping that mirrors the snowy peaks and fjords of Arendelle.

Walt Disney Studios Park combines the excitement of blockbuster franchises, Pixar magic, and behind-the-scenes cinematic wonders, ensuring a memorable experience for visitors of all ages. With its recent expansions and upcoming attractions, the park continues to grow as a premier destination for Disney fans and adventure seekers alike.

CHAPTER 6

Top Attractions and Experiences

A trip to Disneyland Paris is filled with unforgettable attractions, magical shows, and cherished moments with beloved Disney characters. Here's a detailed guide to ensure you make the most of your visit.

Must-Ride Attractions
Both **Disneyland Park** and **Walt Disney Studios Park** boast iconic rides catering to all age groups and adventure levels.
Disneyland Park:
1. **Big Thunder Mountain (Frontierland):**
    - A thrilling roller coaster through a Wild West mining town. Popular for its scenic views and high-speed excitement.
2. **Pirates of the Caribbean (Adventureland):**
    - A dark ride through pirate-infested waters with lifelike animatronics and stunning effects.
3. **Star Wars Hyperspace Mountain (Discoveryland):**
    - A high-speed roller coaster with a galactic theme and immersive Star Wars soundtrack.
4. **Peter Pan's Flight (Fantasyland):**
    - A family-friendly journey over London and Neverland aboard a magical flying pirate ship.
5. **It's a Small World (Fantasyland):**
    - A gentle, whimsical boat ride featuring animatronic dolls representing cultures from around the world.

Walt Disney Studios Park:
1. **The Twilight Zone Tower of Terror:**

- A heart-pounding drop tower with a spooky storyline set in a haunted hotel.
2. **Ratatouille: The Adventure:**
   - A 4D trackless dark ride that shrinks you to the size of a rat as you explore Gusteau's kitchen.
3. **Crush's Coaster:**
   - A spinning roller coaster inspired by *Finding Nemo*, blending underwater visuals with thrilling twists.
4. **Spider-Man W.E.B. Adventure (Avengers Campus):**
   - An interactive ride where guests help Spider-Man capture rogue Spider-Bots using gesture-based technology.
5. **RC Racer (Worlds of Pixar):**
   - A half-pipe roller coaster offering short but exhilarating thrills.

Parades and Shows

Disneyland Paris parades and shows are a highlight of the day, offering colorful performances and beloved characters.

1. **Disney Stars on Parade (Disneyland Park):**
   - A vibrant parade featuring floats themed to iconic Disney movies like *The Lion King*, *Frozen*, and *Toy Story*.
   - Times: Usually in the afternoon. Check the daily schedule.
   - Tip: Arrive early for a good viewing spot along Main Street, U.S.A.
2. **Mickey and the Magician (Walt Disney Studios Park):**

- A live stage show blending music, magic, and appearances from characters like Elsa, Lumière, and the Genie.
3. **Seasonal Parades:**
    - **Halloween Parade:** Features spooky floats and villains like Maleficent and the Evil Queen.
    - **Christmas Parade:** A festive procession with Santa Claus, Disney characters in holiday outfits, and seasonal music.

Meet-and-Greets with Disney Characters

Meeting Disney characters is a magical experience for visitors of all ages.
1. **Classic Disney Characters:**
    - Meet Mickey, Minnie, Donald, and Goofy at designated locations in both parks.
    - Popular spots: **Meet Mickey Mouse** theater in Fantasyland and the character zones in Toon Studio.
2. **Princesses:**
    - Visit the **Princess Pavilion** in Fantasyland to meet characters like Cinderella, Belle, and Snow White.
    - Tip: Check the app for the princess schedule to plan your visit.
3. **Marvel Superheroes (Avengers Campus):**
    - Meet Iron Man, Spider-Man, Black Panther, and other Avengers in themed areas.
    - Heroic performances and interactions add excitement.
4. **Star Wars Characters (Discoveryland):**
    - Encounter Darth Vader and Stormtroopers near the Star Tours attraction.

5. **Seasonal Characters:**
    - During special events, meet characters like Jack Skellington, Santa Claus, or even the Easter Bunny.

Nighttime Spectaculars: Disney Dreams! and Disney Illuminations

Disneyland Paris' nighttime shows are unforgettable experiences combining fireworks, music, and dazzling projections on **Sleeping Beauty Castle**.

1. **Disney Dreams! (Seasonal):**
    - Features iconic Disney songs and scenes projected onto the castle, with water fountains, lasers, and fireworks.
    - Highlights include moments from *The Lion King*, *Peter Pan*, and *Beauty and the Beast*.
    - Tip: This show is seasonal and may alternate with **Illuminations**; check the schedule.
2. **Disney Illuminations (Regular):**
    - A stunning multimedia show with projections, fireworks, and water effects.
    - Highlights include scenes from *Frozen*, *The Little Mermaid*, *Star Wars*, and Marvel films.
    - Timing: Typically scheduled at park closing. Arrive at least 30 minutes early for the best view.
3. **Tips for Viewing:**
    - Best Spot: Directly in front of Sleeping Beauty Castle on Central Plaza.
    - Accessibility: Designated viewing areas for guests with mobility challenges are available—ask Cast Members for assistance.

Disneyland Paris offers endless magic, from world-class attractions to spectacular shows and character experiences. Whether you're chasing thrills, watching parades, or enjoying enchanting nighttime spectacles, every moment is crafted to leave you with lasting memories.

CHAPTER 7

Dining at Disneyland Paris

Disneyland Paris Meal Plans: A Dining Guide for Guests
Planning to stay at a Disney Hotel in Disneyland Paris? Meal plans are a convenient option to enhance your experience. These pre-purchased dining packages cover meals for the entire duration of your stay and apply to all members of your booking. Choose from **Breakfast**, **Half Board**, or **Full Board** meal plans, each offering flexibility and variety to suit your preferences.

Meal Plan Options

1. Breakfast Meal Plan
- **What's Included**:
  One all-you-can-eat breakfast at your Disney Hotel. Options vary by hotel, and at Disney's Davy Crockett Ranch, you'll receive a grab-and-go breakfast.
- **Ideal For**: Guests who want to start their day with a hearty breakfast before exploring the parks.

2. Half Board Meal Plan
- **What's Included**:
  - 1 Breakfast Meal at your Disney Hotel.
  - 1 Lunch or Dinner Meal at a restaurant of your choice.
- **Ideal For**: Those seeking a balance of convenience and flexibility for dining.

3. Full Board Meal Plan
- **What's Included**:
    - 1 Breakfast Meal at your Disney Hotel.
    - 1 Lunch or Dinner Meal.
    - 1 Extra Lunch or Dinner on your departure day.
- **Ideal For**: Guests who want all meals covered throughout the day, ensuring a hassle-free dining experience.

Meal Plan Levels

Your choice of **Standard**, **Plus**, **Extra Plus**, or **Premium** depends on your selected Meal Plan and Disney Hotel.

Extra Plus Treat and Drink

For guests with the **Extra Plus** plan:
- Each night, enjoy a sweet treat and a hot or cold drink from over 35 locations in the Disney Parks and Disney Village (quick service, bars, and grab-and-go).
- Receive one additional drink voucher—alcoholic or non-alcoholic—redeemable at bars or with meals at table service, buffet, and quick service restaurants.

Character Dining Experience

Make your trip even more magical by dining with Disney Characters!
- Swap one lunch or dinner voucher for a **Character Dining Experience**.
- Options include:
    - **Auberge de Cendrillon**
    - **Royal Banquet**
    - **Plaza Gardens Restaurant**

Important Note:
- Valid park tickets are required for dining in the Disney Parks.
- Dining in the Disney Village does not require a park ticket and is open to all.

Meal Plan Availability by Hotel	
Hotel	**Meal Plan Options**
Disney's Hotel Santa Fe	Half Board Standard, Full Board Plus, Full Board Extra Plus
Disney's Davy Crockett Ranch	Half Board Standard, Full Board Plus, Full Board Extra Plus
Disney's Hotel Cheyenne	Half Board Plus, Full Board Plus, Full Board Extra Plus
Disney's Sequoia Lodge	Half Board Plus, Full Board Plus, Full Board Extra Plus
Disney's Newport Bay Club	Half Board Plus, Full Board Plus, Full Board Extra Plus
Disney's Hotel New York – The Art of Marvel	Half Board Plus, Full Board Plus, Full Board Extra Plus
Disneyland Hotel Paris	Half Board Premium, Full Board Premier

Pro Tips for Meal Plans
- **Reserve Early**: Disneyland Paris restaurants are highly popular. Reserve your tables as soon as possible using the Disneyland Paris app or website.

- **Check Restaurant Availability**: Some restaurants may close seasonally or due to maintenance, so verify in advance.
- **Flexible Dining**: Dining in Disney Village is open to all, regardless of park tickets.

With Disneyland Paris meal plans, you can simplify your dining experience, save time, and enjoy a magical variety of meals tailored to your preferences. Whether it's breakfast with Mickey or an evening feast, there's a plan for every guest!

Disneyland Paris Meal Plan Costs

Meal plans at Disneyland Paris offer a convenient way to enjoy dining while staying within your budget. Here's a breakdown of the nightly prices per person based on the type of plan and age group:

Half Board Standard
- **Adult (12+ years)**: £49.32 per night
- **Child (3–11 years)**: £31.39 per night

Full Board Standard
- **Adult (12+ years)**: £67.26 per night
- **Child (3–11 years)**: £40.35 per night

Half Board Plus
- **Adult (12+ years)**: £58.30 per night
- **Child (3–11 years)**: £35.88 per night

Full Board Plus
- **Adult (12+ years)**: £103.14 per night
- **Child (3–11 years)**: £53.81 per night

Full Board Extra Plus
- **Adult (12+ years)**: £134.53 per night

- **Child (3–11 years)**: £71.73 per night

Half Board Premium
- **Adult (12+ years)**: £121.07 per night
- **Child (3–11 years)**: £67.25 per night

Full Board Premium
- **Adult (12+ years)**: £219.72 per night
- **Child (3–11 years)**: £121.07 per night

Key Notes
- Prices are **per night per person** and include meals for the duration of your stay.
- Children aged **3–11 years** enjoy reduced prices, while children under 3 dine for free.
- Meal plan options are flexible and tailored to your hotel and dining preferences.

Whether you opt for Standard, Plus, Extra Plus, or Premium, meal plans offer an excellent way to simplify your dining experience while exploring the magic of Disneyland Paris!

Making Disneyland Paris Dining Reservations

To secure a spot at your favorite Disney restaurant, download the **free Disneyland Paris Mobile App**. While Meal Plans are convenient, they don't guarantee a reservation, so booking in advance is essential. We recommend making reservations as soon as you finalize your stay and Meal Plan. Keep in mind that restaurant availability may vary.

MagicPass and Meal Plans

If you're staying at a Disney Hotel, each guest aged 3 and older will receive a **MagicPass**, which links directly to your Meal Plan for easy dining access.

Kids' Meals

Disney restaurants offer diverse and delicious meal options tailored for kids, including balanced choices that are sure to please. **Highchairs**, **microwaves**, **bottle warmers**, and other amenities are available upon request, depending on availability.

Allergen Information

If anyone in your party has allergies, notify a staff member upon arrival at any Disney Park or Hotel restaurant.
- Staff can provide allergen information for each dish on the menu.
- Although Disney ensures high food preparation standards, cross-contamination is possible.
- Pre-ordering is unnecessary, as allergen-friendly meals are available on-site.
- Disney cannot modify meals to suit specific allergen requests.

Special Dietary Needs

Disneyland Paris caters to various dietary preferences, including **allergen-free**, **vegetarian**, **kosher**, and **halal** meals.
- For kosher or halal meals, call **+33 1 60 30 40 50** at least 48 hours before your reservation (international rates apply).
- Note that orders made between **2 pm on Fridays and 9 am on Mondays** may not meet the 48-hour guarantee.

Important Meal Plan Notes

1. **Meal Coverage:** Meal Plans include the specified number of meals per person (ages 3 and up) for each night of your stay, unless stated otherwise.
2. **Breakfast Options:** Breakfast is typically an **all-you-can-eat buffet**, except at **Disney Davy Crockett Ranch**, where a grab-and-go breakfast bag is provided.
3. **Lunch & Dinner Choices:** Options include **table service**, **all-you-can-eat**, or **quick service** restaurants. At table service spots, adults receive a three-course meal from a set menu, while kids' meals are also pre-set.
4. **Hotel-Specific Meal Plans:** Your hotel determines the available Meal Plan options. The key difference between **Half Board Plus** and **Half Board Standard** lies in the variety of breakfast options.
5. **Upgrades:** Guests can upgrade Meal Plans (e.g., from **Standard** to **Plus**, or from **Plus** to **Extra Plus**).
6. **Availability:** Product availability may vary, and **Character Dining** is subject to availability. While the experience is magical, specific characters, schedules, or experiences may change without notice.
7. **Extra Plus Treats:** The **Extra Plus Treat & Drinks** option is not available at **Disneyland Hotel** restaurants and bars, including **La Table de Lumière** and **Fleur de Lys Bar**.
8. **Exclusions:** Wine pairings, shared drinks, souvenir beverages, and bottles of alcohol are not included in any Meal Plan.

By planning ahead and understanding the details, you can enjoy a seamless and magical dining experience during your Disneyland Paris stay!

Table-Service Restaurants

For a more leisurely and themed dining experience, consider these highly-rated table-service restaurants:

1. **Disneyland Park:**
   - **Auberge de Cendrillon (Fantasyland):**
     - A fairy-tale setting where guests can enjoy French cuisine while meeting Disney Princesses.
     - Menu Highlights: Escargot, beef filet, and seasonal desserts.
   - **Walt's – An American Restaurant (Main Street, U.S.A.):**
     - A tribute to Walt Disney's life, featuring classic American dishes with European influences.
     - Menu Highlights: Lobster rolls, roasted duck, and a variety of gourmet desserts.
2. **Walt Disney Studios Park:**
   - **Bistrot Chez Rémy (Toon Studio):**
     - A Ratatouille-themed restaurant where you feel shrunk to the size of a rat.
     - Menu Highlights: Ratatouille, filet steak, and decadent desserts.
3. **Disney Village:**
   - **The Steakhouse:**
     - Known for premium cuts of meat and Chicago-style ambiance.
     - Menu Highlights: Grilled ribeye, BBQ ribs, and cheesecake.

- **Annette's Diner:**
  - A retro 1950s diner offering burgers, milkshakes, and American comfort food.

Quick-Service and Snacks

Perfect for those on the go, quick-service eateries offer a range of satisfying and themed options.

1. **Disneyland Park:**
   - **Casey's Corner (Main Street, U.S.A.):**
     - Hot dogs, fries, and American classics served in a baseball-themed setting.
   - **Hakuna Matata Restaurant (Adventureland):**
     - African-inspired dishes like chicken skewers and seasoned rice.
   - **Pizzeria Bella Notte (Fantasyland):**
     - Italian-inspired meals such as pizza, pasta, and tiramisu.
2. **Walt Disney Studios Park:**
   - **Restaurant en Coulisse (Front Lot):**
     - Quick bites like burgers, chicken nuggets, and fries in a Hollywood-themed eatery.
   - **La Cantina (Avengers Campus):**
     - Marvel-themed snacks and casual meals.
3. **Snacks and Street Food:**
   - **Popcorn and Mickey-shaped Pretzels:** Available at carts throughout both parks.
   - **Churros and Crepes:** Popular options found at snack kiosks.

- **Seasonal Treats:** Look out for special items during Halloween, Christmas, and other events.

Character Dining Experiences

Dining with Disney characters is a magical way to interact with your favorites while enjoying a meal.

1. **Auberge de Cendrillon (Disneyland Park):**
   - Meet Disney Princesses in an elegant castle setting. Ideal for families and special celebrations.
2. **Plaza Gardens Restaurant (Disneyland Park):**
   - Enjoy a buffet-style meal with visits from classic characters like Mickey, Minnie, and Goofy.
   - Best for breakfast and early lunch reservations.
3. **Disneyland Hotel Restaurants (Temporarily Closed for Renovation):**
   - Once reopened, expect high-end character dining experiences featuring rare characters.
4. **Tips for Character Dining:**
   - Book in advance, as these experiences are very popular and fill up quickly.
   - Bring an autograph book and camera to capture the magic.

Food Allergies and Special Diets

Disneyland Paris is accommodating to guests with dietary restrictions, including allergies, vegetarian, vegan, and gluten-free needs.

1. **Allergy-Friendly Options:**

- Many restaurants offer allergy menus. Inform the staff of your dietary requirements upon arrival.
- Pre-packaged allergy-friendly meals are available at select locations.

2. **Vegan and Vegetarian Options:**
   - **Hakuna Matata Restaurant:** Vegan options such as plant-based skewers.
   - **Annette's Diner:** Offers a plant-based burger.
   - Check menus in advance or inquire with staff about substitutions.

3. **Halal and Kosher Options:**
   - Some restaurants offer halal-certified meals; inquire in advance.
   - Kosher meals are available upon request but require prior notice (at least 48 hours).

4. **Tips:**
   - Use the Disneyland Paris app to filter dining options by dietary requirements.
   - Speak directly with chefs or managers if you have severe allergies or need specific accommodations.

Insider Tips for Dining Reservations

1. **When to Book:**
   - Reservations open 60 days in advance; book early for popular restaurants and character dining experiences.

2. **How to Book:**
   - Use the official Disneyland Paris app or website.
   - Call the dining reservation line if you need assistance or have special requests.

3. **Timing Tips:**
   - Dine during non-peak hours (early lunch or late dinner) to avoid crowds.
   - For nighttime shows like Disney Illuminations, book a dinner reservation that allows you to finish in time to secure a viewing spot.
4. **Walk-Ins:**
   - While walk-ins are accepted at some locations, availability is limited. Plan ahead to avoid disappointment.

Disneyland Paris offers a magical culinary journey, with options to suit every palate, age group, and budget. From indulging in fine dining to grabbing a Mickey-shaped snack, the variety of experiences ensures your meals are as memorable as the attractions!

CHAPTER 8

Shopping and Souvenirs Guide at Disneyland Paris

Disneyland Paris offers an enchanting shopping experience with its array of themed shops, unique merchandise, and magical souvenirs to commemorate your visit. Here's a complete guide to navigating the shopping experience at the parks while keeping your budget in check.

1. Top Shops in the Parks
a. Disneyland Park
1. **Emporium** (Main Street, U.S.A.)
    - The largest store in Disneyland Park, offering a wide variety of Disney-themed merchandise, including clothing, plush toys, homeware, and more.
    - *Best For*: Classic Disney souvenirs and collectibles.
2. **Thunder Mesa Mercantile Building** (Frontierland)
    - Specializes in Western-themed merchandise, inspired by Big Thunder Mountain and the wild west.
    - *Best For*: Cowboy hats, Western apparel, and Frontierland memorabilia.
3. **La Chaumière des Sept Nains** (Fantasyland)
    - A fairytale-themed shop featuring princess costumes, accessories, and toys.

- Best For: Fans of Disney princesses and fairytales.
4. **Star Traders** (Discoveryland)
   - Offers Star Wars and space-themed merchandise, including lightsabers, apparel, and collectibles.
   - Best For: Star Wars enthusiasts and sci-fi fans.

b. Walt Disney Studios Park
1. **Les Légendes d'Hollywood** (Front Lot)
   - A Hollywood-style boutique offering apparel, jewelry, and Disney-themed luxury items.
   - Best For: Fashion-forward Disney fans.
2. **Chez Marianne (Souvenirs de Paris)** (Toon Studio)
   - A charming shop offering Parisian-style Disney merchandise, including Ratatouille-themed items.
   - Best For: Unique French-Disney crossover souvenirs.
3. **Tower Hotel Gifts** (The Twilight Zone Tower of Terror)
   - Features spooky and thrilling memorabilia inspired by the iconic attraction.
   - Best For: Fans of the Tower of Terror and thrilling experiences.

c. Disney Village
- **World of Disney**: The ultimate shopping destination outside the parks, offering the widest range of Disney merchandise.
- **Disney Fashion**: Specializes in trendy Disney clothing and accessories for adults and children.
- **The LEGO Store**: Features exclusive Disney-themed LEGO sets and building kits.

2. Unique Souvenirs and Merchandise
a. Exclusive to Disneyland Paris
- **Minnie Ears and Spirit Jerseys**: Special designs available only at Disneyland Paris.
- **French-Inspired Merchandise**: Items like Ratatouille-themed kitchenware and Mickey macarons.
- **Park-Specific Collectibles**: Limited edition pins, artwork, and ornaments featuring park attractions.

b. Customizable Keepsakes
- **Engraved Items**: Personalize jewelry, keychains, and glassware at select stores.
- **Custom Mickey Ears**: Choose your design and have your name embroidered at locations like La Boutique du Château.

c. Attraction-Themed Merchandise
- **Big Thunder Mountain**: Western apparel and themed toys.
- **Pirates of the Caribbean**: Pirate hats, swords, and nautical décor.
- **It's a Small World**: Globally-inspired souvenirs like dolls and home accessories.

3. Tips for Budget-Friendly Shopping
a. Plan Your Budget
- Decide on a spending limit before your visit and stick to it.
- Prioritize must-have items like a pair of Minnie ears or a signature pin.

b. Look for Deals
- Check for **seasonal sales** or discounts at shops, especially in Disney Village.

- Annual Passholders often enjoy discounts on merchandise.

c. Souvenir Ideas Under €20
- Keychains, magnets, and mugs make affordable and memorable keepsakes.
- Collectible pins are small, budget-friendly items with designs for every taste.

d. Bring Your Own Gear
- To save money, consider bringing your own autograph book, glow sticks, or costumes for kids instead of purchasing them in the parks.

e. Shop Smartly
- Shop early in the day to avoid last-minute purchases that may exceed your budget.
- Consider purchasing from Disney Village at the end of your visit to avoid carrying bags all day.

f. Use Discounts and Promotions
- Some credit cards and travel agencies offer discounts for Disneyland Paris merchandise.
- Keep an eye out for bundle deals, such as "buy 2, get 1 free" promotions on select items.

Final Tips for a Magical Shopping Experience
- **Use Disney's Shopping Service**: If you're staying at a Disneyland hotel, have your purchases delivered directly to your room.
- **Take Advantage of Unique Offerings**: Look for items exclusive to Disneyland Paris that you won't find at other Disney parks.
- **Capture Memories**: Consider small, practical souvenirs like photo frames or notebooks that combine utility with sentimentality.

CHAPTER 9

Disneyland Paris for Kids

Disneyland Paris is a magical destination for children of all ages, offering enchanting rides, dedicated services, and facilities designed to make a family visit stress-free and enjoyable. Here's a detailed guide to ensure your little ones have the best experience.

Rides and Attractions for Little Ones

Disneyland Paris is filled with attractions tailored to younger guests, from gentle rides to immersive experiences.

In Disneyland Park:
1. **Fantasyland:**
    - **"it's a small world"**
        - A gentle boat ride through a colorful, musical celebration of global cultures.
        - Perfect for toddlers and young kids.
    - **Peter Pan's Flight:**
        - Fly over London and Neverland in a magical pirate ship.
        - A family favorite with a captivating story and visuals.
    - **Dumbo the Flying Elephant:**
        - Soar through the sky on Dumbo's back, with the ability to control your ride height.
        - Ideal for small children who love whimsical rides.
    - **Le Carrousel de Lancelot:**

- A beautifully themed carousel where kids can ride majestic horses.
2. **Adventureland:**
    - **Le Passage Enchanté d'Aladdin:**
        - A walkthrough attraction showcasing scenes from *Aladdin*.
        - A calm, visual experience great for young adventurers.
3. **Main Street, U.S.A.:**
    - **Horse-Drawn Streetcars:**
        - A slow-paced ride in vintage-style streetcars, offering a relaxed journey through the heart of Disneyland Park.
4. **Discoveryland:**
    - **Buzz Lightyear Laser Blast:**
        - A family-friendly interactive shooting game where kids help defeat Emperor Zurg.

In Walt Disney Studios Park:
1. **Worlds of Pixar:**
    - **Slinky Dog Zigzag Spin:**
        - A spinning ride that's gentle and fun, featuring Slinky Dog from *Toy Story*.
    - **Cars ROAD TRIP:**
        - A scenic ride featuring beloved characters and iconic scenes from *Cars*.
2. **Toon Studio:**
    - **Flying Carpets Over Agrabah:**
        - A magical ride where kids control the height of their carpet.
    - **Ratatouille: The Adventure:**

- While thrilling for older kids, its visuals and immersive story make it accessible for younger ones as well.

Baby Care Centers and Child-Friendly Services

Disneyland Paris is equipped with facilities to cater to families with babies and toddlers.

1. **Baby Care Centers:**
   - Locations:
     - **Disneyland Park:** Near the entrance to Main Street, U.S.A.
     - **Walt Disney Studios Park:** Near Studio Services.
   - Features:
     - Private nursing rooms, changing tables, highchairs, and microwaves for warming bottles or food.
     - Supplies such as diapers, baby food, and wipes are available for purchase.

2. **Child-Friendly Amenities:**
   - **Restaurants:** Most restaurants offer highchairs, kid-friendly menus, and bottle warming facilities.
   - **Lost Children:**
     - If a child gets separated, inform a Cast Member immediately. Lost children are taken to the Baby Care Center until reunited with their guardians.

3. **Parent Swap Service:**
   - Allows one parent to wait with a child while the other rides, then swap without having to queue again.

Stroller Rentals and Accessibility

For families with small children, Disneyland Paris provides convenient stroller rental services and maintains a high level of accessibility.

1. **Stroller Rentals:**
    - Available at both Disneyland Park and Walt Disney Studios Park.
    - Location:
        - **Disneyland Park:** Near the entrance on Main Street, U.S.A.
        - **Walt Disney Studios Park:** Near the entrance.
    - Cost:
        - Approximately €25 per day (a refundable deposit may be required).
    - Features:
        - Lightweight and easy to maneuver strollers designed for park use.
        - Tip: Bring your own stroller if it's more comfortable for your child.
2. **Accessibility:**
    - Rides:
        - Many attractions offer accessible queues and accommodations for families with young children.
    - Elevators and Ramps:
        - Both parks are equipped with ramps and elevators for strollers and wheelchairs.
3. **Tips for Families:**
    - Bring a lightweight stroller cover or blanket for added comfort during naptime.

- Label rented strollers with your family name for easy identification.

Disneyland Paris has thoughtfully designed its attractions and services to cater to young visitors, ensuring a magical experience for both children and their parents. From enchanting rides to practical facilities like Baby Care Centers and stroller rentals, the parks make it easy for families to focus on creating unforgettable memories.

Accessibility and Services

Disneyland Paris is dedicated to making the experience enjoyable and accessible for all guests, providing a range of services and facilities to accommodate various needs. Here's a comprehensive overview of what you need to know:

Accessibility for Guests with Disabilities

Disneyland Paris is committed to inclusivity, offering services to ensure that everyone, regardless of ability, can enjoy the magic.

1. **Access Cards for Guests with Disabilities:**
    - **Priority Access Card:** For guests with permanent disabilities, providing priority access to attractions, shows, and character meet-and-greets.
    - **Easy Access Card:** For guests with temporary disabilities or conditions requiring simplified access.
    - How to Obtain:
        - Visit City Hall (Disneyland Park) or Studio Services (Walt Disney Studios Park) with documentation proving the disability (e.g., medical certificate).
2. **Ride Accessibility:**
    - Many attractions are designed to accommodate wheelchairs or have specific boarding assistance.
    - Attractions are categorized by access types:
        - Walk-on access.
        - Transfer from a wheelchair to a ride vehicle.

- Accompanied access for those needing additional assistance.
    - Look for accessibility symbols on maps and signage.
3. **Wheelchair Rentals:**
    - Available for rent near the entrances of both parks.
    - Cost: Approximately €25 per day with a refundable deposit.
    - Personal wheelchairs are welcome throughout the parks.
4. **Hearing and Visual Assistance:**
    - **Hearing Disabilities:**
        - Induction loops available at specific attractions and Guest Services locations.
        - Sign Language interpretation is provided on certain days for shows; inquire in advance for availability.
    - **Visual Disabilities:**
        - Guide dogs are welcome throughout the parks, with designated rest areas.
        - Tactile maps and Braille menus are available upon request.
5. **Companion Assistance:**
    - Reduced admission is offered for one companion assisting a guest with a disability.

Language Considerations (English vs. French)
While Disneyland Paris is located in France, it is a multilingual destination, ensuring a seamless experience for international visitors.
1. **Park Language:**

- Most signage, maps, and announcements are provided in both French and English.
- Attractions often feature a mix of both languages, with some offering subtitles or translations.

2. **Cast Members:**
   - Many Cast Members speak multiple languages, including English, Spanish, German, and Italian.
   - Look for language badges on their name tags to identify their spoken languages.

3. **Language Tips for Non-French Speakers:**
   - Use the Disneyland Paris mobile app, which is available in multiple languages, including English.
   - Carry a translation app for off-site interactions if you're exploring beyond the parks.

Mobile App and Park Navigation

The Disneyland Paris mobile app is an essential tool for navigating the parks and enhancing your visit.

1. **Key Features:**
   - **Interactive Maps:** Locate attractions, dining, restrooms, and shows with ease.
   - **Wait Times:** Real-time updates for ride and character meet-and-greet queues.
   - **Show Schedules:** View performance times and parade routes.
   - **Mobile Reservations:** Book dining experiences directly through the app.
   - **Digital Tickets:** Use the app to store and scan your park tickets for easy entry.

2. **Navigation Tips:**

- Enable location services for personalized guidance within the parks.
- Use the app to set reminders for shows, dining reservations, or key attractions.

Wi-Fi, Charging Stations, and Lockers

Modern conveniences like Wi-Fi and charging stations ensure a hassle-free experience for tech-savvy visitors.

1. **Wi-Fi Access:**
   - Free Wi-Fi is available throughout Disneyland Park, Walt Disney Studios Park, and Disney Village.
   - Tip: Connect to "Disneyland Paris" Wi-Fi upon arrival for seamless browsing and app usage.
2. **Charging Stations:**
   - Portable charging kiosks are located in key areas around the parks.
   - Charging lockers are available for hire, allowing you to recharge devices securely.
   - Tip: Bring a portable power bank for convenience, especially during long days in the parks.
3. **Lockers:**
   - Locations: Near park entrances in Disneyland Park and Walt Disney Studios Park.
   - Cost: Varies by size; small, medium, and large lockers are available.
   - Tip: Use lockers to store bulky items or seasonal clothing so you can move around the park unencumbered.

Disneyland Paris goes above and beyond to provide accessible services and modern amenities, ensuring that all guests, regardless of ability or language, can enjoy the magic. With thoughtful planning and the help of dedicated resources, you can focus on creating unforgettable memories!

CHAPTER 10

Tips for Beating the Crowds

Disneyland Paris is a popular destination that attracts millions of visitors each year, so navigating the parks efficiently is key to making the most of your visit. Here's a detailed guide to help you avoid long lines and crowded areas.

Using Genie+ or FastPass Alternatives
Disneyland Paris no longer offers the traditional FastPass system but has introduced paid alternatives to help you skip the lines.
1. **Disney Premier Access:**
    - **What It Is:**
        - A paid service allowing you to access shorter lines for select attractions.
    - **How It Works:**
        - Purchase access via the Disneyland Paris mobile app or at in-park kiosks.
        - Choose from two types of passes:
            - **Disney Premier Access One:** Buy entry for specific attractions individually.
            - **Disney Premier Access Ultimate:** Provides access to all eligible attractions once during the day.
    - **Eligible Attractions:**
        - Includes popular rides like *Big Thunder Mountain*, *Hyperspace Mountain*, and *Ratatouille: The Adventure*.

2. **Tips for Using Premier Access Effectively:**
   - Purchase early in the day, as availability can sell out quickly.
   - Prioritize high-demand rides to save the most time.

Early Entry and Extra Magic Hours
Staying at an official Disneyland Paris hotel gives you early access to the parks, a major advantage in avoiding crowds.
1. **Extra Magic Time:**
   - **What It Is:**
     - Hotel guests and certain Annual Pass holders can enter the parks up to 1 hour before the general public.
   - **Eligible Attractions:**
     - Not all attractions are open, but popular ones like *Peter Pan's Flight*, *Buzz Lightyear Laser Blast*, and *Ratatouille* typically are.
2. **Benefits:**
   - Experience headliner attractions with little to no wait.
   - Enjoy quieter walkways and photo opportunities without large crowds.
3. **Tips for Early Entry:**
   - Arrive at least 30 minutes before Extra Magic Time begins to maximize your advantage.
   - Head to the most popular rides first, such as *Big Thunder Mountain* or *Avengers Assemble: Flight Force*.

Quiet Times and Less Busy Seasons

Knowing when to visit can make a huge difference in crowd levels and overall experience.

1. **Quiet Times to Visit:**
   - **Off-Peak Seasons:**
     - January to mid-March (after holiday crowds).
     - Mid-September to mid-November.
   - **Mid-Week Days:**
     - Tuesdays through Thursdays are typically quieter than weekends.
   - **Early Mornings and Late Evenings:**
     - Parks are less crowded right after opening and an hour before closing.
2. **Less Busy Seasons:**
   - **Low Season:**
     - Avoid major holidays, school vacations (both French and European), and long weekends.
   - **Mid-Season:**
     - May and early June see moderate crowds with pleasant weather.
3. **Crowded Seasons to Avoid:**
   - **Summer (July-August):** Peak season with the highest crowds.
   - **Christmas and New Year's:** Magical but extremely busy.

Additional Tips for Beating Crowds

1. **Arrive Early:**
   - Being at the park gates 30–45 minutes before opening ensures you're ahead of the main crowd.

2. **Stay Late:**
   - Many visitors leave after the nighttime spectaculars. If the park is still open, use this time to enjoy shorter queues.
3. **Plan Meals Wisely:**
   - Eat during off-peak hours (e.g., early lunch at 11:30 AM or late dinner after 8:00 PM) to avoid restaurant queues.
4. **Single Rider Lines:**
   - Use single rider queues on attractions like *RC Racer* or *Indiana Jones* for faster access if you don't mind riding alone.
5. **Leverage the Disneyland Paris Mobile App:**
   - Monitor real-time wait times and adjust your plans accordingly.
   - Enable notifications for updates on ride openings and schedule changes.
6. **Split Your Visit Across Two Days:**
   - Allocate one day for Disneyland Park and another for Walt Disney Studios Park to enjoy a more relaxed pace.
7. **Explore During Parades and Shows:**
   - Many visitors gather for parades and nighttime spectaculars, making this an ideal time to visit popular rides.

By strategically planning your visit, taking advantage of early entry and services like Disney Premier Access, and timing your trip during less busy periods, you can maximize your time at Disneyland Paris while minimizing the stress of crowds.

CHAPTER 11

Budgeting for Disneyland Paris

A trip to Disneyland Paris can be a magical experience, but it's essential to plan your budget carefully to avoid unexpected expenses. Here's a detailed guide to help you estimate costs, save money, and make the most of your visit without overspending.

Cost Breakdown: Tickets, Accommodation, Food, and Extras

Here's a typical breakdown of expenses for a Disneyland Paris trip:

1. **Park Tickets:**
   - **Single-Day Tickets:**
     - Prices range from €60–€120 per adult, depending on the season and day of the week (off-peak vs. peak).
   - **Multi-Day Tickets:**
     - Two-day tickets: €150–€200 per adult.
     - Three-day tickets: €200–€270 per adult.
   - **Add-Ons:**
     - Disney Premier Access: €10–€18 per ride (or €140 for the Ultimate Pass).
   - Tip: Book tickets online in advance to lock in lower prices and avoid on-site surcharges.
2. **Accommodation:**
   - **Official Disney Hotels:**

- Budget options (e.g., Disney's Hotel Santa Fe): From €150 per night.
- Mid-range options (e.g., Disney's Newport Bay Club): From €250 per night.
- Luxury options (e.g., Disneyland Hotel): €500+ per night.
- **Partner Hotels and Nearby Options:**
  - Partner hotels: From €100–€200 per night.
  - Central Paris hotels: From €80–€300, depending on location and quality.

3. **Food and Drinks:**
    - **Table-Service Restaurants:** €30–€50 per meal per person.
    - **Quick-Service Restaurants:** €12–€20 per meal per person.
    - **Snacks and Drinks:** €4–€10 for items like popcorn, churros, or coffee.
    - Tip: Budget €40–€70 per person per day for meals.

4. **Extras:**
    - **Souvenirs and Merchandise:** €10–€100, depending on items (e.g., keychains vs. exclusive collectibles).
    - **PhotoPass+:** €75 for unlimited professional photos.
    - **Transportation:**
      - Shuttle services: €20–€30 per person.
      - Train tickets (RER): €7.60 one way from central Paris.
      - Parking: €30 per day for cars.

Money-Saving Tips and Hacks

Visiting Disneyland Paris on a budget doesn't mean compromising the magic. Here are some ways to save money:

1. **Book Early:**
   - Tickets and accommodations are usually cheaper when booked several months in advance.
   - Take advantage of early-bird offers and seasonal discounts on the official Disneyland Paris website.
2. **Travel During Off-Peak Seasons:**
   - Visit during January–March or September–November for lower ticket and hotel prices.
   - Weekdays are typically cheaper than weekends.
3. **Stay Off-Site:**
   - Partner hotels or accommodations in nearby towns (e.g., Val d'Europe) often cost less and include shuttle services to the parks.
4. **Pack Snacks:**
   - Bring your own snacks and water bottles to avoid paying premium park prices.
   - Disneyland Paris allows outside food, provided it's not in large coolers.
5. **Choose Multi-Day Tickets:**
   - Multi-day tickets provide better value per day compared to single-day tickets.
6. **Skip the Premier Access:**
   - Plan your day strategically to avoid needing Premier Access, saving up to €140 per person.
7. **Utilize Discounts:**
   - Check for discounts for students, seniors, or group bookings.

- Some credit cards and travel memberships offer cashback or additional perks.
8. **Free Water Stations:**
    - Refill water bottles at free fountains available throughout the parks to avoid buying bottled water.

Budget-Friendly Dining and Shopping
1. **Dining on a Budget:**
    - **Quick-Service Restaurants:**
        - Opt for counter-service meals at places like *Toad Hall Restaurant* or *Colonel Hathi's Pizza Outpost*. Meals range from €12–€15.
    - **Kids' Meal Deals:**
        - Kid-friendly meal options are often filling and include a drink and dessert, typically under €10.
    - **Picnic Areas:**
        - Use the picnic area near the park entrance to enjoy your own packed meals.
2. **Shopping on a Budget:**
    - **Souvenirs:**
        - Choose smaller items like pins, magnets, or mugs, which are typically under €15.
    - **Sales and Discounts:**
        - Look out for seasonal sales or discounts at stores in Disney Village.
    - **Off-Site Shopping:**
        - Visit shops in Val d'Europe for Disney-themed merchandise at lower prices.

3. **Meal Plans:**
    - Disneyland Paris offers dining plans that can save money if booked in advance:
        - **Standard Plan:** Covers buffet meals.
        - **Plus Plan:** Includes table-service dining.
        - **Premium Plan:** Offers access to the most exclusive restaurants, such as Auberge de Cendrillon.
    - Tip: Calculate whether a meal plan matches your budget and dining preferences.

Budgeting for Disneyland Paris doesn't mean sacrificing the experience. With thoughtful planning, early bookings, and a few cost-saving hacks, you can enjoy the magic of the parks without overspending.

CHAPTER 12

Exploring Beyond Disneyland Paris

While Disneyland Paris offers an enchanting escape, the surrounding region has plenty to explore, from world-class shopping to historical and cultural landmarks. Here's a detailed guide to making the most of your time beyond the parks.

Val d'Europe and La Vallée Village Shopping
Located just minutes from Disneyland Paris, Val d'Europe and La Vallée Village are must-visit destinations for shopping enthusiasts.
1. **Val d'Europe Shopping Mall:**
    - **Overview:**
        - A sprawling mall featuring over 160 shops, restaurants, and entertainment options.
    - **Top Stores:**
        - High-street brands like Zara, H&M, and Sephora.
        - Specialized stores for toys and souvenirs.
    - **Dining Options:**
        - A variety of restaurants and cafés, including quick bites and sit-down meals.
    - **Grocery Shopping:**

- Auchan supermarket offers affordable food and drinks, perfect for stocking up if you're staying nearby.
    - **Location:**
        - Easily accessible via RER A train, one stop from Disneyland Paris.
2. **La Vallée Village Outlet Mall:**
    - **Overview:**
        - A luxury outlet shopping destination offering discounts on premium brands.
    - **Top Brands:**
        - Gucci, Prada, Lacoste, Michael Kors, and more.
    - **Savings:**
        - Discounts of up to 60% on designer items.
    - **Experience:**
        - A charming open-air village layout with boutique-style stores.
    - **Tips:**
        - Visit early in the day to avoid crowds.
        - Check their website for seasonal sales and exclusive offers.

Day Trips to Paris and Versailles

Disneyland Paris's proximity to Paris and Versailles makes day trips to these iconic destinations a breeze.

1. **Paris:**
    - **Travel Time:**
        - 35–40 minutes via RER A train to central Paris.
    - **Top Attractions:**

- **Eiffel Tower:** Marvel at Paris's most famous landmark and enjoy panoramic views from its top.
- **Louvre Museum:** Explore one of the world's largest art museums, home to the *Mona Lisa*.
- **Notre-Dame Cathedral:** Admire the stunning Gothic architecture of this historic cathedral (exterior currently accessible due to restoration).
- **Montmartre and Sacré-Cœur:** Stroll through this bohemian district and visit the iconic basilica.
    - **Tips for a Day in Paris:**
        - Plan your itinerary around 2–3 key attractions to maximize your time.
        - Purchase skip-the-line tickets for popular sites in advance.

2. **Versailles:**
    - **Travel Time:**
        - Approximately 1.5 hours via RER A train to the Versailles-Château station.
    - **Top Attractions:**
        - **Palace of Versailles:** Explore the opulent rooms, including the Hall of Mirrors.
        - **Gardens of Versailles:** Stroll through the manicured gardens, fountains, and sculptures.
        - **Trianon Palaces:** Visit the Grand Trianon and Marie Antoinette's Petit Trianon for a more intimate look at royal life.

- **Tips for a Day in Versailles:**
  - Wear comfortable shoes; the palace and gardens are expansive.
  - Visit during the week to avoid large weekend crowds.

Other Attractions Near Disneyland Paris

1. **Sea Life Aquarium (Val d'Europe):**
   - **Overview:**
     - A family-friendly aquarium located within Val d'Europe.
   - **Highlights:**
     - Features over 5,000 marine animals, including sharks, rays, and sea turtles.
     - Interactive exhibits like touch pools for kids.
   - **Location:**
     - 5 minutes from Disneyland Paris by shuttle or RER train.
2. **Parc des Félins:**
   - **Overview:**
     - A wildlife park dedicated to the conservation of big cats.
   - **Highlights:**
     - Home to species like tigers, lions, and cheetahs, with large natural habitats.
   - **Travel Time:**
     - Approximately 40 minutes by car from Disneyland Paris.
3. **Provins – A Medieval Town:**
   - **Overview:**

- A UNESCO World Heritage Site known for its well-preserved medieval architecture.
    - **Highlights:**
        - Visit the historic ramparts, Caesar's Tower, and medieval-themed shows.
    - **Travel Time:**
        - Around 1 hour by car or train.
4. **Château de Fontainebleau:**
    - **Overview:**
        - A stunning royal château surrounded by lush forests.
    - **Highlights:**
        - Features elaborate Renaissance and classical interiors.
    - **Travel Time:**
        - Approximately 1.5 hours by car or train from Disneyland Paris.

Tips for Exploring Beyond Disneyland Paris
1. **Plan Transportation:**
    - Use the RER train for efficient and affordable travel to Paris and nearby destinations.
    - If exploring more remote areas, consider renting a car.
2. **Combine Destinations:**
    - Pair Val d'Europe shopping with a visit to La Vallée Village or the Sea Life Aquarium for a full day.
3. **Pack Smart:**
    - Bring a day bag with essentials like water, snacks, and maps, especially for day trips.

4. **Allocate Time Wisely:**
    - Start early to make the most of your day, especially when visiting Paris or Versailles.

Exploring beyond Disneyland Paris adds a layer of richness to your trip, blending the magic of Disney with shopping, history, and culture. Whether you prefer retail therapy, iconic landmarks, or hidden gems, the region offers something for everyone.

CHAPTER 13

FAQs and Insider Tips

Commonly Asked Questions
1. What is the best time to visit Disneyland Paris?
- Weekdays during off-peak seasons (mid-January to mid-March, mid-April to mid-May, or mid-September to mid-November) tend to have smaller crowds.
- Arrive early to make the most of Extra Magic Time if staying at a Disney Hotel.

2. Can I bring my own food and drinks?
- Outside food and drinks are generally not allowed inside the parks. Exceptions are made for dietary needs, baby food, or small snacks.
- Water bottles and snacks are permitted for personal use.

3. What are the must-have apps and resources?
- Download the **Disneyland Paris App** for real-time updates on attraction wait times, show schedules, and dining options.
- Use **Disney Premier Access** for shorter queues at select attractions.

4. How does transportation work?
- The RER A train connects Paris to Disneyland Paris in about 40 minutes.
- Free shuttles are available between Disney hotels and the parks.

5. Is there Wi-Fi in the parks?
- Complimentary Wi-Fi is available throughout Disneyland Paris.

Cultural Differences to Be Aware Of
1. Dining Culture
- Meals in France are leisurely. Don't expect fast service, especially during sit-down meals.
- Dinner often begins later in the evening, around 7:30 PM or later.

2. Smoking Areas
- Smoking is more common in Europe. Dedicated smoking areas are located throughout the park. Be aware of these designated zones.

3. Personal Space
- Crowds can feel different as people in Europe tend to stand closer in queues than in other cultures.

4. Tipping Practices
- Tipping is not obligatory in France but is appreciated for exceptional service.

5. Language Expectations
- While many Cast Members speak English, learning a few French phrases can enhance your experience.

Tips from Disneyland Paris Veterans
1. Planning Your Day
- Begin with popular attractions such as **Big Thunder Mountain** or **Ratatouille: The Adventure** to avoid long wait times later.
- Use the **Single Rider Line** to skip the standby queue for certain attractions.

2. Dining Tips
- Book table-service restaurants in advance to avoid disappointment. Reservations can be made up to 2 months before your visit.

- Try unique dishes and treats like **Mickey-shaped waffles** or the **Ratatouille-inspired menu** at Chez Rémy.

3. Parade and Show Viewing
- Arrive at least 30 minutes early for parades and nighttime shows to secure a good viewing spot.
- Consider watching parades from less crowded areas, such as near the entrance of Fantasyland.

4. Budget Hacks
- Purchase tickets in advance for better pricing and avoid buying on-site.
- Consider staying at partner hotels for budget-friendly accommodations while still being close to the parks.

5. Insider Tips for Families
- Use the **Baby Switch** service to take turns riding attractions without requiring both parents to queue again.
- Pack essentials like ponchos, sunscreen, and a portable phone charger for a smoother day.

6. Unique Disneyland Paris Experiences
- Explore **Alice's Curious Labyrinth** for a whimsical and quieter park experience.
- Visit the **Dragon's Lair** beneath Sleeping Beauty Castle—an attraction unique to Disneyland Paris.

By keeping these FAQs and tips in mind, you'll have a magical and seamless Disneyland Paris adventure!

CHAPTER 14

Emergency Information

First Aid and Medical Assistance
- **First Aid Stations**:
    - Located in both **Disneyland Park** (near Central Plaza) and **Walt Disney Studios Park** (near Studio Services).
    - Staffed with trained medical personnel to provide assistance for minor injuries, illnesses, or emergencies.
- **Medications**:
    - If you need to store medication that requires refrigeration, notify a Cast Member at the First Aid Station.
    - Over-the-counter medication is not sold on-site, so bring what you need in advance.
- **Emergencies**:
    - For serious emergencies, contact any Cast Member, who will alert emergency services immediately.
    - AED (Automated External Defibrillators) are available in the parks and can be accessed by trained staff.

Lost and Found Services
- **Location**:
    - The main **Lost and Found Office** is in **Disneyland Park**, near the park entrance.
- **Process**:

- o Report a lost item as soon as possible to increase the chances of recovery.
- o Items found in the park are cataloged, and if unclaimed after a specific period, they are donated or disposed of.
- **Tips**:
  - o Label your personal belongings with your name and contact details for easier identification.
  - o If you lose something after leaving the parks, you can still contact Lost and Found via the **Disneyland Paris website**.

Contact Numbers and Useful Apps
- **Emergency Contact Numbers**:
  - o Local Emergency Number (Fire, Police, Ambulance): **112**.
  - o Disneyland Paris General Information: **+33 1 60 30 60 53**.
  - o First Aid Assistance (on-site): Ask any Cast Member for help.
- **Guest Relations**:
  - o For park-related inquiries or emergencies, visit the **City Hall** in Disneyland Park or the **Studio Services** in Walt Disney Studios Park.

Useful Apps
- **Disneyland Paris App**:
  - o Features:
    - Real-time attraction wait times and schedules for parades and shows.
    - Dining reservations and mobile food ordering.

- ▪ Maps of both parks for easy navigation.
- **Google Maps**:
  - o Use for finding your way to Disneyland Paris or locating nearby services.
- **Translation Apps**:
  - o Apps like **Google Translate** or **SayHi** can help communicate with staff or locals if you need assistance in French.
- **RATP App**:
  - o The official app for Paris public transportation, including the RER A train to Disneyland Paris.
- **WhatsApp**:
  - o Ideal for staying in touch with your group or contacting Guest Services, as many prefer instant messaging over calls.

By keeping this emergency and assistance information handy, you'll be prepared for unexpected situations and can focus on enjoying your magical Disneyland Paris adventure!

CHAPTER 15

Printable Resources

Park Maps and Layout
- **Disneyland Park Map**:
    - Includes a detailed layout of the park's themed lands, including **Main Street, U.S.A.**, **Adventureland**, **Frontierland**, **Fantasyland**, and **Discoveryland**.
    - Marked locations for attractions, dining, restrooms, First Aid, and Guest Services.
    - Available at park entrances or online via the **Disneyland Paris website**.
- **Walt Disney Studios Park Map**:
    - Highlights areas such as **Front Lot**, **Toon Studio**, **Production Courtyard**, and **Marvel Avengers Campus**.
    - Features attraction wait times and show schedules when accessed through the Disneyland Paris app.
- **Interactive Digital Maps**:
    - Use the **Disneyland Paris app** for GPS-enabled navigation.
    - Offers live updates on attraction wait times and dining availability.

Daily Planner Template
Plan your day effectively with this simple, customizable daily planner template:

Time	Activity	Notes
8:00 AM - 9:00 AM	Arrive at Park	Early Magic Time for hotel Guests.
9:00 AM - 11:00 AM	Popular Attractions	Visit high-demand rides first.
11:00 AM - 12:00 PM	Snacks/Shopping	Explore nearby boutiques.
12:00 PM - 1:00 PM	Lunch	Pre-reserve dining locations.
1:00 PM - 3:00 PM	Afternoon Attractions	Use Disney Premier Access if needed.
3:00 PM - 4:00 PM	Shows/Parades	Check app for performance times.
4:00 PM - 6:00 PM	Evening Rides	Revisit favorite attractions.
6:00 PM - 7:00 PM	Dinner	Enjoy dining with themed experiences.
8:00 PM Closing	Fireworks/Light Show	Plan for an early viewing spot.

Print this table or customize it for your specific park visit.

Packing Checklist

Ensure you have everything you need for a comfortable and enjoyable trip with this handy checklist:

Essential Documents:
- Tickets (printed or digital)
- Park reservations
- Photo ID
- Hotel booking confirmation

Clothing and Accessories:
- Comfortable shoes for walking

- Weather-appropriate clothing (e.g., jackets, hats, raincoats)
- Extra socks
- Disney-themed attire for fun photos

Tech and Gadgets:
- Portable phone charger
- Camera or smartphone for photos
- Plug adapter (if traveling internationally)
- Pre-downloaded Disneyland Paris app

Health and Safety:
- Face masks (if required)
- Hand sanitizer
- Medications
- Band-aids for blisters

For Families with Kids:
- Stroller (or plan to rent one)
- Snacks and refillable water bottles
- Autograph book and pen for character meet-and-greets
- Favorite toys or distractions for long waits

Extras:
- Small backpack or fanny pack
- Reusable shopping bag
- Sunscreen and sunglasses
- Umbrella or poncho for unexpected weather

Print this checklist to ensure you're prepared and have everything you need to fully enjoy your Disneyland Paris adventure!

1-Week Detailed Itinerary for Disneyland Paris and Nearby Attractions

Day 1: Arrival and Disney Village Exploration
- **Morning**:
  - Arrive in Paris and travel to **Disneyland Paris Resort** (via train, shuttle, or taxi).
  - Check into your Disney hotel or nearby accommodation.
  - Take time to rest and unpack.
- **Afternoon**:
  - Head to **Disney Village** for shopping and dining.
  - Explore stores like **World of Disney** and **Disney Fashion** for souvenirs.
  - Enjoy lunch at **Annette's Diner** or **Rainforest Café**.
- **Evening**:
  - Relax and enjoy live music or shows in Disney Village.
  - Optional: Watch a movie at the **Gaumont Cinema**.
  - Return to your hotel to rest for a full day ahead.

Day 2: Disneyland Park (Main Park)
- **Morning**:
  - Enter the park early with **Extra Magic Time** (available for Disney hotel Guests).
  - Start with **Main Street, U.S.A.**, then head to **Fantasyland** to experience iconic rides like **Peter Pan's Flight**, **It's a Small World**, and **Mad Hatter's Tea Cups**.

- **Afternoon**:
  - Move to **Adventureland** for **Pirates of the Caribbean** and **Indiana Jones and the Temple of Peril**.
  - Enjoy lunch at **Captain Jack's – Restaurant des Pirates**.
- **Evening**:
  - Explore **Discoveryland** for attractions like **Star Wars Hyperspace Mountain** and **Buzz Lightyear Laser Blast**.
  - Find a spot on **Main Street** for the **Disney Illuminations** nighttime spectacular.

Day 3: Walt Disney Studios Park

- **Morning**:
  - Begin at **Front Lot** and take photos with Hollywood-themed backdrops.
  - Experience **Ratatouille: The Adventure** and **Crush's Coaster** in **Toon Studio**.
- **Afternoon**:
  - Visit the **Marvel Avengers Campus** for attractions like **Avengers Assemble: Flight Force**.
  - Have lunch at **PYM Kitchen** or **Stark Factory**.
- **Evening**:
  - Watch the **Studio D show** or experience thrilling rides like **The Twilight Zone Tower of Terror**.
  - Return to your hotel for a restful evening.

Day 4: Paris City Highlights
- **Morning**:
    - Take a train (RER A) to central Paris (approx. 40 minutes).
    - Visit the iconic **Eiffel Tower** and enjoy panoramic views of the city.
- **Afternoon**:
    - Explore the **Louvre Museum** or **Musée d'Orsay** for art and history.
    - Have lunch in a nearby Parisian café.
- **Evening**:
    - Stroll along the **Seine River** or visit **Notre-Dame Cathedral**.
    - Return to Disneyland Paris Resort in the evening.

Day 5: Disneyland Park (Themed Lands and Hidden Gems)
- **Morning**:
    - Focus on **Frontierland**: Ride **Big Thunder Mountain** and explore **Phantom Manor**.
    - Visit **Adventure Isle** and explore the caves and suspension bridges.
- **Afternoon**:
    - Take a break at **Hakuna Matata Restaurant**.
    - Enjoy entertainment like the **Disney Stars on Parade**.
- **Evening**:
    - Revisit favorite attractions or shop for exclusive merchandise at **Emporium** on Main Street.

- Have dinner at **Walt's – an American Restaurant**.

Day 6: Nearby Attractions
- **Morning**:
  - Visit **Val d'Europe**, a nearby shopping center with premium outlets and designer stores.
  - Explore **La Vallée Village** for luxury shopping.
- **Afternoon**:
  - Stop by **Sea Life Aquarium** in Val d'Europe for an educational experience.
  - Have lunch in one of the local restaurants or cafés.
- **Evening**:
  - Relax at your hotel or return to **Disney Village** for a leisurely dinner.

Day 7: Farewell Day
- **Morning**:
  - Enjoy a character breakfast at your hotel or **Plaza Gardens Restaurant** in Disneyland Park.
  - Take last-minute photos with Disney characters and enjoy a few final rides.
- **Afternoon**:
  - Spend time at **Disney Village** for any last-minute souvenir shopping.
- **Evening**:
  - Depart from Disneyland Paris to your next destination.

Tips for Your Visit:
- Use the **Disneyland Paris app** for real-time updates on wait times and dining reservations.
- Consider **Disney Premier Access** for shorter lines on popular rides.
- Pack comfortable shoes and weather-appropriate clothing for long days in the parks.
- Book tickets and reservations for Paris attractions in advance to save time.

Enjoy a magical week at Disneyland Paris and its surrounding attractions!

ALL DISNEY CHARACTERS AND FRIENDS

Classic Disney Characters:
- **Mickey Mouse**
- **Minnie Mouse**
- **Donald Duck**
- **Daisy Duck**
- **Goofy**
- **Pluto**

Disney Princesses:
- **Cinderella**
- **Jasmine**
- **Ariel**
- **Tiana**
- **Aurora**
- **Belle**
- **Rapunzel**
- **Snow White**

These princesses often greet guests at the Princess Pavilion in Fantasyland.

Disneyland Paris

Pixar Characters:
- **Woody**
- **Buzz Lightyear**
- **Remy** (from *Ratatouille*)

Star Wars Characters:
- **Darth Vader**
- **Chewbacca**

Marvel Superheroes:
- **Spider-Man**
- **Captain America**
- **Iron Man**

Other Beloved Characters:
- **Baloo** (from *The Jungle Book*)
- **Captain Jack Sparrow** (from *Pirates of the Caribbean*)
- **Alice** (from *Alice in Wonderland*)
- **Aladdin**
- **Winnie the Pooh**

Please note that character appearances can vary daily, and some may be available only during special events or seasons. For the most accurate and up-to-date information on character meet-and-greet locations and times, it's recommended to consult the official Disneyland Paris app or website before your visit.

MINNIE MOUSE

DONALD DUCK

GOOFY

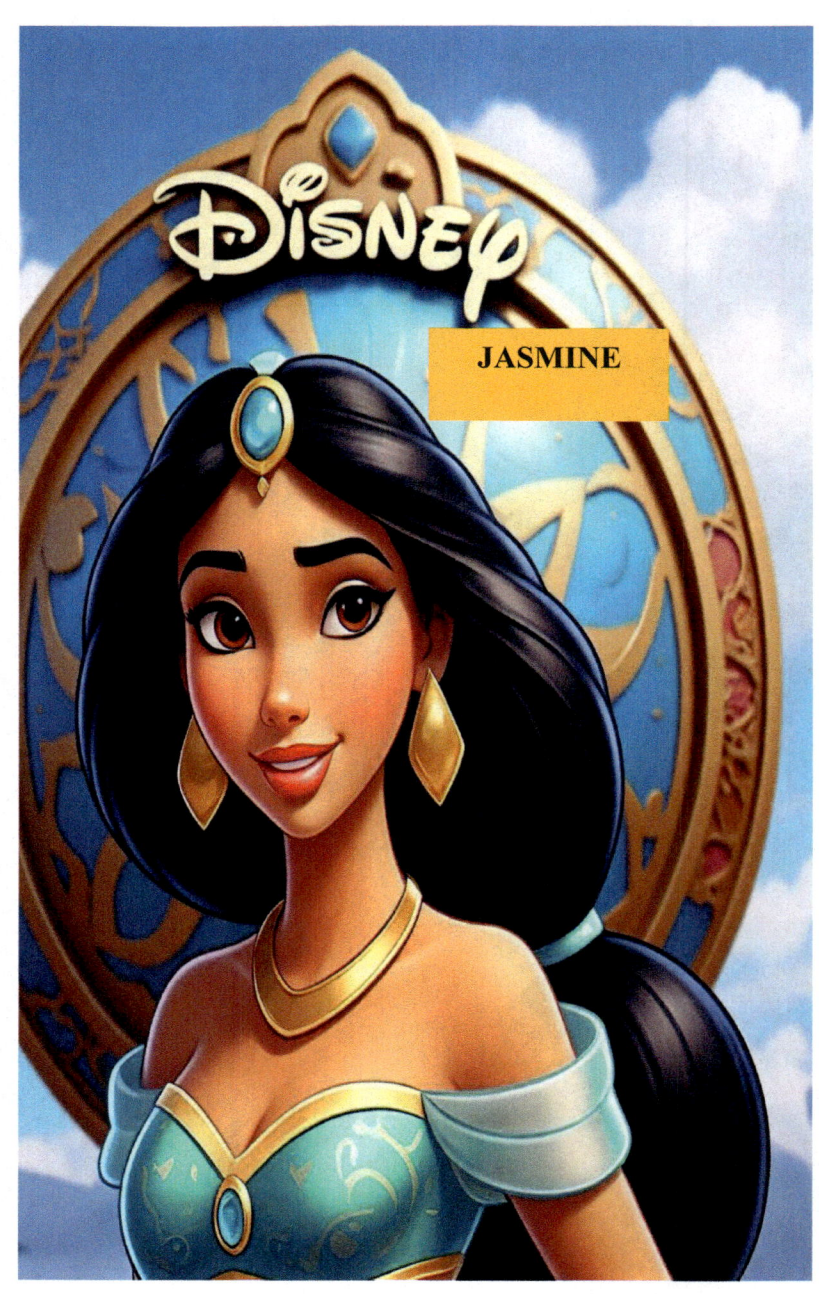

AURORA & MINNIE

BELLE & MINNIE

SNOW WHITE

RAPUZEL

TRAVEL
PLANS

Printed in Dunstable, United Kingdom

74849758R00087